T0312914

Meaning: A Very Short Introduction

VERY SHORT INTRODUCTIONS are for anyone wanting a stimulating and accessible way into a new subject. They are written by experts, and have been translated into more than 45 different languages.

The series began in 1995, and now covers a wide variety of topics in every discipline. The VSI library currently contains over 750 volumes—a Very Short Introduction to everything from Psychology and Philosophy of Science to American History and Relativity—and continues to grow in every subject area.

Very Short Introductions available now:

Available soon:

For more information visit our website

www.oup.com/vsi/

Emma Borg and Sarah A. Fisher

MEANING

A Very Short Introduction

Great Clarendon Street, Oxford, OX2 6DP,
United Kingdom

Oxford University Press is a department of the University of Oxford.
It furthers the University's objective of excellence in research, scholarship,
and education by publishing worldwide. Oxford is a registered trade mark of
Oxford University Press in the UK and in certain other countries

Published in the United States of America by Oxford University Press
198 Madison Avenue, New York, NY 10016, United States of America

British Library Cataloguing in Publication Data
Data available

Library of Congress Control Number: 2024940948

ISBN 9780192866547

Printed and bound by
CPI Group (UK) Ltd, Croydon, CR0 4YY

The manufacturer's authorised representative in the EU for product safety is Oxford
University Press España S.A. of el Parque Empresarial San Fernando de Henares,
Avenida de Castilla, 2 – 28830 Madrid (www.oup.es/en).

Acknowledgements

We would like to thank Nat Hansen, Joe Oppenheimer, Claire Lewis, and an anonymous reviewer for providing very helpful comments on earlier versions of the book, which helped to much improve the final version. Thanks are also due to Tara Werger and Latha Menon, who provided excellent support from the Press.

Sarah Fisher's work on the project was supported by UKRI (grant reference MR/V025600/1). Emma Borg's work was supported by a Leverhulme Trust Major Fellowship (MRF-2019-031). Both authors would like to express their thanks to these funders.

Contents

List of illustrations

Chapter 1
Meaning and language

In 1953 a UK citizen, Derek Bentley, was executed for murder. The facts of his offence (explored in the 1991 film *Let Him Have It*) were as follows: Bentley, then aged 18, was involved in an attempt to rob a warehouse with an accomplice, Christopher Craig (aged 16). However, police were alerted during the attempted break in and, when they arrived on the scene, one policeman (Frederick Fairfax) was able to grab hold of Bentley. At this point, Christopher Craig drew the gun he was carrying (Bentley was armed only with a knuckle-duster, which Craig had given to him, and which Bentley never attempted to use). All agreed that Fairfax shouted, 'Give me the gun lad', however the next point was disputed. According to the prosecution, but denied by the defence, Bentley then uttered a key phrase: 'Let him have it, Chris.' Craig fired the gun, hitting and injuring Fairfax. A short time later he shot and killed another policeman, Sidney Miles.

Although Bentley's legal team denied that he had ever uttered the words 'Let him have it', at trial they also argued that, even were Bentley believed to have uttered the key phrase, the meaning of that sentence in that context would simply have been *Let the policeman have the firearm, Chris*. On the contrary, the prosecution team argued that the correct interpretation was an incitement to violence; what Bentley meant, the prosecution alleged, was *Shoot him, Chris*.

In the end, Craig and Bentley were both found guilty of the murder of Sidney Miles, under the legal principle of Joint Enterprise. Craig, as he was under 18 at the time of the offence, was sentenced to be detained at Her Majesty's Pleasure (eventually being released 10 years later). Bentley, on the other hand, was sentenced to death. Following an unsuccessful appeal and despite a public outcry, he was executed by hanging in January 1953. Following a 40-year campaign by his family, Bentley received a posthumous pardon in 1993 and his conviction was finally overturned in 1998.

There are many troubling aspects to this case, but one of the core worries clearly concerns meaning. How were the jury supposed to decide the correct meaning of the alleged utterance? In this context, did 'Let him have it' express a de-escalating request for Craig to hand over the weapon or was it the inciting call for the gun to be fired? What features could the jury have looked to, and was the judgement they made the right one? In order to answer questions like these we need to know more about *meaning*. In particular, we need to know more about how linguistic items (like words, sentences, and utterances) come to be meaningful. These are the kinds of issues we want to explore in this book, but to start with we need to ask more questions about what exactly is meant by 'meaning'.

The meaning of 'meaning'

In English, 'meaning' is a very broad term with many senses. We can ask about the meaning of natural phenomena ('Do the approaching clouds *mean* it's going to rain?', 'Does that mark *mean* she was bitten by a snake?') or of cultural phenomena ('What does that ringing bell *mean*?', 'What's the *meaning* of this painting?'). Relatedly, we can ask about the meaning of a word or sentence ('What does "phantasmagorical" mean?', 'What does "Der Hund ist wild" mean in English?'). We can also ask what *people* mean when they do or say things (if Naoki rolls his eyes, or says 'Someone is late again', we might wonder, 'What did he *mean* by that?'). Finally, we can ask extremely profound questions, like 'What is the *meaning* of life?' or 'Is existence *meaningless*?' This book focuses primarily on a question about meaning which underlies each of those above, namely, *'What is it for something to have meaning?'* So while, sadly, we won't get as far as asking about the meaning of life, we will explore the nature of meaning itself.

Human societies have one particularly important device for expressing and sharing meaning, namely *language*. Accordingly, this book will concentrate first and foremost on *meaning in language*. Since our words are paradigm examples of things which have meaning, it makes good sense to begin by thinking about them. Moreover, the meaning we capture and share through language plays a pivotal role in our interactions with other people and the world around us. Think of all the many things you have been told over the course of your life, by parents, teachers, friends, and colleagues. Think about how you use language in your day-to-day life, to buy things, make plans, share your experiences, and express your ideas. Imagine trying to do all of that without language! Language greases the wheels of human society so routinely and inconspicuously that we forget how remarkable it really is—and what a crucial role it plays in thinking and communicating in meaningful ways.

Our route into the vast topic of meaning, then, is similar to the one voiced by the philosopher P. F. Strawson in his Inaugural Lecture (entitled 'Meaning and Truth') at Oxford University in 1969:

> What is it for anything to have a *meaning* at all, in the way, or in the sense, in which words or sentences or signals have meaning? What is it for a particular sentence to have the meaning or meanings it does have? What is it for a particular phrase, or a particular word, to have the meaning or meanings it does have?

As we will see, questions about meaning arise particularly clearly and concretely in relation to language. Thus we will be interested in exactly how languages allow meaning to be captured, expressed, and understood. However, it should be kept in mind that meanings are not simply identical to linguistic expressions. Consider, for instance, pairs of synonyms like 'small' and 'little', or 'puma' and 'cougar'. Here we have two different words with one and the same meaning. On the flipside, we often encounter words that have multiple meanings. For example 'stick' can be a verb meaning *to adhere*, or a noun meaning *a twig*.

Likewise, we have to be careful to hold sentences apart from what they mean. Again, this is clearest where different sentences, stringing together different words, share a single meaning (e.g. 'The cat ate the mouse' in English and 'Die Katze hat die Maus gefressen' in German); or where one sentence has multiple meanings (as in 'I teased the cat with a toy', which is ambiguous between *I used a toy to tease the cat* and *The cat I teased had a toy*). Those who study language often refer to the meanings expressed by sentences as 'contents' or 'propositions', but we will generally stick with talk of 'meanings'.

Although we will be focusing on meaning in language, many of the ideas we encounter can be applied more generally, to the meanings of other kinds of signs and symbols (like gestures or facial expressions), as well as to thoughts and other (natural or human-made) entities. We'll indicate as we go along some of the ways in which what we say generalizes and thus by the end of the book you'll have the tools you need to switch your focus from meaning in language to meaning in any other field.

To begin our discussion, it will be helpful to think a bit more about what counts as a language in the first place. Although our focus in what follows will be on natural human languages (like English, French, Arabic, or Mandarin), these are certainly not the only possible candidates for languages. We might, for example, classify non-human animal communication systems as languages, treating monkey calls, bird songs, and perhaps even bee dances, as (primitive) forms of language. In a different direction, we might extend the idea of a language to artificial systems, like mathematical or logical systems, computer programs, or AI instructions. What these kinds of languages have in common is that they are complex systems, composed of symbols which get manipulated in various ways, where the aim is, it seems, to capture and convey information. However, while there are clear affinities, there are also important differences. Seeing how natural human languages differ from these other systems reveals some interesting features that matter for an investigation of meaning.

Meaning and artificial languages

First, let's consider artificial languages (e.g. mathematics, or computer programming languages like Java and Python). These symbolic systems do share some key features with natural human languages. For instance, artificial languages reuse and recombine parts of complex expressions to create new and different messages (that is to say, they contain basic, word-like symbols which can be used in different, complex combinations to form new instructions). However, there are also some significant differences between artificial languages and natural languages, and the most important of these concerns whether the symbols manipulated within artificial languages possess *meaning* at all.

To see this, imagine that I write a Java program which contains the following rule:

1. class Dog implements Animal

My Java program thus contains a class *Dog* and the information that this class interfaces with the category *Animal*. So, is my Java program *about* dogs and animals? Is the meaning of the Java symbol 'Dog' the same as the meaning of the English word 'dog'? And indeed, does the symbol 'Dog' in (1) really *mean* anything at all?

Initially, we might think that of course the signs used in the computer program are meaningful, either because the programmer who introduced them in the first place meant something by them or because we, as users of the system, take them to mean something. On this line of thought, the signs manipulated by computational systems have meaning because *we* (ordinary language users) mean something by them. While this seems right, note that such a move doesn't really help if we are interested in the question of how meaning gets into a system in the first place: the fact that the symbols used by artificial systems *preserve* the meaning instilled in them by programmers or users doesn't help us answer the more fundamental question of how those symbols became meaningful initially. Philosophers have introduced a distinction to capture this point: they distinguish between 'derived aboutness' (or, in more technical language, 'derived intentionality') and the more fundamental notion of 'original aboutness' ('original intentionality'). It is then often argued that while the symbols of a computational system can inherit meaning from their program and/or users, it is original intentionality that matters from the perspective of an investigation of meaning per se. The thought here is that people can represent things because they have minds, but inanimate objects, like words, maps, pictures, computer symbols, and tree rings, can represent things only because they are used in a certain way by people.

Furthermore, although 'Dog' and 'dog' look superficially very similar, there are reasons to think that the symbols manipulated by an artificial system play a very different role from the words manipulated by ordinary speakers. For what a symbol means seems to be irrelevant to the operations of computational systems. To see this note that, when we look at the above line of Java script, we could decide to interpret the symbols in it in lots of different ways without this changing the way that the program behaves.

For instance, we could decide to interpret the Java script term 'Dog' as referring to cars and 'Animal' as referring to the property of being a vehicle and, at least as far as line (1) goes, this wouldn't make any difference. While interpreting the computer symbols in this way would no doubt be annoying and confusing for others, making this kind of idiosyncratic decision wouldn't change anything with regards to how the program runs. Computational systems, according to many theorists, are not sensitive to the meaning properties of the symbols they manipulate.

John Searle produced a famous thought experiment which is pertinent here. Searle asked us to consider a person who is locked inside a windowless room. This person receives input from the outside world in the form of scraps of paper with messages written on them in a language they don't understand (in Searle's original example the envisaged language was Chinese, hence the thought experiment is known as 'the Chinese Room'). The room also contains a huge look-up table which matches incoming symbols with a further set of symbols, which the person copies out onto another piece of paper and then sends out of the room (see Figure 1).

I don't know what any of these signs mean. I'm just following rules written in English (which I do understand). These rules just tell me how to pair incoming marks with the marks I should output.

狗是动物吗？
〔Are dogs animals?〕

是的, 狗是动物〕
〔Yes, dogs are animals〕

If the input stream looks like:
狗是动物吗
You should output the following symbols:
是的, 狗是动物

1. **John Searle's 'Chinese Room' thought experiment.**

Although the person in the room doesn't realize this, the input symbols are questions in Chinese and the matching output symbols are answers to these questions, again in Chinese. If the look-up table has been well constructed, Searle argues, it would appear to the casual observer that the person in the room understands Chinese—after all, asked a question in Chinese, they respond with an appropriate answer. Yet, intuitively, this is *just* an appearance—the person doesn't understand the meaning of the symbols they are manipulating at all. For instance, an incoming question might ask whether dogs are animals, and the outgoing response might state that dogs are indeed animals, but the person in the room is simply oblivious to this, as they don't understand the Chinese writing they are looking at. All they see are meaningless marks.

Searle contends that the Chinese Room mirrors what computers do: all a machine is capable of is manipulating meaningless marks that we, the users or programmers, invest with meaning. This idea has a long history. For instance, Charles Sanders Peirce, a philosopher who lived in the late 19th and early 20th centuries, stressed the crucial role that users of signs play, holding that 'Nothing is a sign unless it is interpreted as a sign.'

Meanwhile, Hilary Putnam, in his 1981 book *Reason, Truth and History*, focused on the role that producers (rather than interpreters) play in endowing signs with meaning. Putnam asked us to imagine an ant crawling across a patch of sand, going backwards and forwards to a food source and leaving a trail where it has moved. Imagine that the line the ant traces turns out to look just like the profile of Winston Churchill (see Figure 2).

Putnam's question was then, 'Has the ant produced a picture of Churchill?' Intuitively, he says, the ant has not. It is just pure chance that the line it has left bears this resemblance; the ant wasn't *trying* to draw Churchill. Although we (as observers) could subsequently choose to see the line as an image of Churchill, we

2. Hilary Putnam's thought experiment suggesting that the intentions behind the production of a sign matter for meaning.

would be investing the line with a property it didn't have when it was produced. What Searle, Peirce, and Putnam are all pushing on, in their different ways, is the crucial role that *people* play in enabling bits of the world to be meaningful, by intending them to stand for other things, or taking them to do so.

The comparison between natural human languages and artificial languages, like computer programs, highlights the fact that natural language expressions have full-blooded content; what we will call *semantic* properties. Thought experiments like Searle's Chinese Room or Putnam's ant-in-the-sand demonstrate how the purely formal properties of a symbol or sign can come apart from its semantic properties. Although the line of Java coding in (1) above has some of the formal properties of human languages, it seems to lack crucial meaning properties that depend on having rich connections with the world. While the symbols manipulated in artificial languages may be *treated* as if they have meaning, any meaning they have is entirely derivative, at least if we accept Searle's argument. The symbols come to mean something only if

9

we choose to connect them with the natural communication systems used by people situated in the world.

The computer which instantiates our Java program, even though it includes line 1, won't (without *much* further work) be able to recognize a dog or categorize the barking, furry beast in front of it as an animal when Fido walks by. That is to say, the computer won't output the term 'dog' in the presence of dogs, won't know that dogs are common pets, or that if Fido is a dog then Fido probably barks, etc. In short, the computer won't be able to do many (if any) of the suite of things we expect of children who grasp the English word 'dog'. Despite rapid technological advancement, it doesn't seem as if this gap will be filled simply by writing more rules for the computer, specifying the properties of dogs and animals more fully, or giving the computer access to more dog-related data (though this is a controversial and very lively research topic). In the absence of the appropriate kind of connection between a symbol and the thing(s) it is supposed to be about, the idea that the symbol 'Dog' in (1) could really mean the same as the English word 'dog' is highly questionable.

Finally, however, we should think about artificial systems which interface with their users not using the symbols of special, technical programming languages, like Java, but using the words of ordinary, natural languages. Recently there have been huge (and very well publicized) advances in the use of computers for what is called 'natural language processing'. It is common now to interact with chatbots and other Artificial Intelligence systems which utilize English or another natural human language. Systems such as OpenAI's ChatGPT (in its various different versions), Google's Gemini, Microsoft's Bing, and OpenAI's DALL-E system (which creates realistic images or art from a natural language description) take as input and return as output things which we, as ordinary users of linguistic or pictorial signs and symbols, certainly recognize as meaningful. Furthermore, it can be very hard to resist the idea that we are dealing with an ordinary communicative

When was the Battle of Hastings?

The Battle of Hastings took place on October 14, 1066. It was a pivotal battle in English history and marked the beginning of the Norman Conquest of England. The Norman forces, led by William the Conqueror, defeated the English army led by King Harold II. This battle had a profound impact on the history and culture of England.

3. Screenshot of exchange with ChatGPT.

partner when we are interacting with a chatbot. For instance, if I ask you, 'When was the Battle of Hastings?' and you reply '1066', I can use your answer to advance my understanding (assuming I think you are reliable on this kind of topic) and I can happily go on to convey this piece of information to others. Yet exactly the same things hold of the answer ChatGPT gives to the same question (Figure 3).

Just as with an interaction with a human, it seems that I can use ChatGPT's answer to advance my understanding (indeed ChatGPT's answer tells me more than my human interlocutor did) and that I can then go on to convey this information to others.

However, there are reasons to think things are a bit more complicated than they appear to be here and the question of whether these systems can be said to 'mean what they say' arises in particularly stark ways. For, as many commentators have noted, it is clear that ChatGPT and similar systems can't (currently) be relied on to convey factual information. Instead, the systems spit out falsehoods and inaccurate claims (in what appear to be pretty mysterious ways). Furthermore, the systems sometimes go on to support a false claim by 'fabricating evidence'. To see this, take a shocking case reported in *The Washington Times* on 5 April 2023 (by Pranshu Verma and Will Oremus): as part of a research study, a lawyer in California asked ChatGPT to generate a list of legal scholars who had been accused of sexual harassment. One name on the list was law professor Jonathan Turley, who, the chatbot reported, had made sexually suggestive comments and attempted to touch a student while on a class trip to Alaska. ChatGPT went on to cite an article in *The Washington Post* in March 2018 as the source of the information. As Verma and Oremus note, however: 'The problem: No such article existed. There had never been a class trip to Alaska. And Turley said he'd never been accused of harassing a student.'

What cases like these (and other, less serious fabrications) make clear is that these systems seem to be working in a way that is different to human speakers. Large Language Models (like ChatGPT) operate on vast datasets (the dataset for training GPT-4 is estimated to consist of 100 trillion parameters, more than five times larger than the training data for GPT-3, for instance) and they utilize this information base (via what is known as a 'deep learning architecture') to create something called a 'vector' for each word (crudely, a statistical weighting which captures how a token word in a context is associated with other words in the database). To do this, Large Language Models utilize a process known as 'Reinforcement Learning with Human Feedback': to start with, the system engages in unsupervised learning where it 'makes guesses' about the next word to appear in a sentence, where that sentence already appears in its database. The system then checks to see if its guess is right. If it is, the route which led to that guess is reinforced. If the guess is incorrect, the route is suppressed.

For instance, say the training dataset for a version of ChatGPT contains the sentence 'To be or not to be, that is the question.' During training, the system might block out the final word of this sentence and make (initially random) guesses about what word appears in that slot. The system then reveals the actual answer and compares its guesses. Then it has another go, and another go, and another go, and so on, each time altering the weights that it is internally assigning to expressions to reflect what it is learning. By iterating this kind of process an extraordinarily large number of times on an extraordinarily large number of sentences, the system eventually homes in on words which lie in the same vector space.

That is to say, it homes in on words which have similar sets of relations to all the other words in the language. So, for instance, it might home in on words like 'question', 'issue', and 'matter', as good guesses for the final word of this sentence, while coming to minimize guesses involving words with very different vectors (like 'politician' or 'red'). Finally, following this kind of massive, extended, unsupervised learning, there is then usually a further period where human feedback is used to fine-tune the system, helping it to select the most appropriate continuations from a range of suggestions made by the system.

The result of all this learning is that the system becomes able to take a sentence of natural language as input and, using internally stored information, output a response which fits naturally within the conversational context. At no point in the operation of the system, however (at least at time of writing), is there a concern for reporting what is true or accurate. Furthermore (just as with our Java program), questions can be asked about whether Large Language Models are really in the business of dealing with *meaning* at all.

One, sceptical, school of thought here argues that (just as with our Java program) the symbols used by ChatGPT and fellow models have nothing more than derived meaning and that Large Language Models are entirely insensitive to the meaning we invest in the symbols they manipulate. To say that ChatGPT *meant* that the Battle of Hastings happened in 1066 in the exchange above is nothing more than loose talk (akin to saying that 'the calculator *says* that 8×15 is 120'). Sceptics about the idea that Large Language Systems are picking up on anything like the meaning of words argue that these systems are simply playing a big numbers game to deliver likely continuations of a sentence (a kind of auto-completion system on steroids). In a phrase made famous by the computational linguist Emily Bender and colleagues (in a paper in 2021), they argue that Large Language Models are nothing more than 'stochastic parrots'—probability-based mechanisms which just parrot our words back to us without any sensitivity to the fact that those words actually mean something. Despite the very impressive results they deliver, this school of thought holds that it would be a mistake to assume that Large Language Models are doing the same thing as ordinary speakers and the impression that their outputs count as meaningful (in anything more than a derived or loose sense) should be rejected.

An underlying thought here is that there is a practical aspect to meaning in language, which depends on knowing how to interact with other people and other things. Some philosophers have thought that the knowledge involved in grasping the semantic properties of expressions must be rather substantial. So, for example, someone might only be deemed to understand the meaning of 'The Taj Mahal' if they can recognize or even navigate to the building being named. Other philosophers have allowed that our knowledge can be much thinner: it might be enough to take 'The Taj Mahal' to name a building somewhere, or even just to be a name (of *something*). Either way, the semantic knowledge involved in understanding language is, from this perspective, held to go beyond a purely formal competence of the kind Large Language Models undoubtedly have, whereby they operate on symbolic inputs and produce other symbolic outputs. According to this view we should expect an account of meaning to tell us how meaning in language is grounded through our human engagement with others and with the world.

Not everyone, however, adopts the sceptical perspective on the operations of Large Language Models (or, indeed, on the languages of artificial systems in general). An opposing school of thought maintains that artificial systems are in fact capable of capturing, processing, and conveying meaning (that they are, in a phrase, 'semantic engines' not merely 'syntactic engines'). One version of this anti-sceptical approach points to the fact (agreed by both sceptic and non-sceptic alike) that Large Language Models are pattern spotters par excellence, tracking, recording, and utilizing the incredibly complex relationships between the words in a language. Yet we might think that it is in fact these patterns (rather than any connection to things in the world) that give words their meaning. This idea has a long history in linguistics (in a field known as 'distributional semantics'). As the linguist John Rupert Frith (writing in the 1950s) suggested in a famous slogan: 'You shall know a word by the company it keeps.'

From this perspective, knowing the meaning of a word crucially involves knowing what other words it tends to appear with: grasping the meaning of 'dog', for instance, involves knowing that it is more likely to appear alongside words like 'barks', 'pet', and 'animal' than alongside words like 'justice', 'feathered', or 'gills'. If we think that meaning does reside in these kinds of language-internal relations, then we may well be more optimistic about the idea that artificial systems like Large Language Models are capturing, and are sensitive to, the meanings of words (not merely their formal properties).

The jury is very much out at the moment on how we should think about and characterize the operations of Large Language Models, but thinking about what we should say about them helps to bring into focus the most fundamental questions that will concern us in what follows: what is meaning and where does meaning in language come from? What is it that makes 'dog' mean *dog* in my mouth, but (arguably) not when it appears in the output of a simple computer program or perhaps even in the output of a Large Language Model?

Meaning and animal languages

Let's return now to the question of how human and non-human animal languages compare. One big difference concerns the degree of flexibility, or what we might term the 'expressive power', of human languages over their animal counterparts. Animal languages, as far as we can tell, have a degree of rigidity and inherent limitation which are not present in human languages.

To see this, consider the call system of vervet monkeys, which contains several different alarm calls, issued according to the kind of threat the monkey perceives. So, for instance, these monkeys give different calls to signify a predator approaching on the ground versus a predator approaching from the sky. The resulting repertoire of alarm calls might be taken to constitute a rudimentary language but we should be clear that they are very simple signs. Each kind of call correlates with just one specific kind of stimulus (e.g. ground predator).

Crucially, vervet monkeys do not take elements of their calls and combine or recombine them with other signs to convey different sorts of messages. The monkeys don't, for instance, reuse parts of their 'predator on the ground' call to convey messages like *food* on the ground' or 'predator *by the tree*' in the way that human languages allow. (We should note that, although widely accepted, the claim that animal languages lack combinatorial signs has been disputed, with some researchers, such as the linguist Philippe Schlenker, arguing that, on the contrary, there is evidence of combinatorial meanings in animal languages.) Furthermore, unlike human languages, animal languages don't seem to exploit the capacity to use signs in ways that transcend the natural environment, as it were; animals don't, as far as we can tell, speak about music or mathematics, or use metaphor or metonymy (metonymy involves picking out a concept by referring to something closely related to it, e.g. saying 'the crown' to talk about royalty).

Comparing human and animal languages allows us to see that an important feature of human (and artificial) languages is their complex internal structures, which allow messages to be built up of re-combinable parts. This structure—known as *syntax* (or *grammar*)—turns out to underpin a distinctive capacity for flexible and creative communication.

Here is a sentence you have probably never encountered before:

Every tall girl petted a purple cat.

How did you manage to grasp its meaning? It is not that you have a comprehensive list of every possible past, present, and future English sentence stored ready-made in your head, pairing each of those sentences with some peculiar kind of object we call its meaning. (The philosopher W. V. O. Quine referred to this kind of model as 'the myth of the museum', where we think of meanings as being like objects on display in a museum, each one labelled with a sentence of a natural language.) Instead, our ability to spontaneously produce and understand new sentences has a much more plausible explanation, based on linguistic structure. Human languages are *compositional*: the meaning of a complex whole (like a sentence) is determined by the meaning of its simpler parts (e.g. the words it contains) and the way that those parts are put together. Our languages have 'hierarchical' or 'recursive' syntax, allowing the basic parts to be combined in novel ways, with those novel constructions themselves becoming available for further combinations. Once you know the meanings of the parts and the meanings of different combinatory structures you hold the key to a whole new world of meaning.

Imagine a child who learns the English word 'ball'. They will be able to use that word to point out balls in their environment. The child will also acquire the ability to convey lots of other things as well: depending on what other linguistic signs they know, they might be able to say that they want the ball, or that the ball is red or round, etc. In general, when a child learns a new name for an object, they acquire not just the ability to indicate the presence of that kind of object (the kind of skill a vervet monkey might be thought to have) but they are also able to combine the name with other words they know, in order to express and understand an apparently open-ended number of new ideas.

Now think again about the sentence 'Every tall girl petted a purple cat.' Even though you hadn't encountered it before, you could work out its meaning because you know the meanings of the individual words, and the effects of putting them together in a particular way. For example, the colour adjective 'purple' appears directly before the noun 'cat'. According to the rules of English, 'purple' is modifying 'cat', so you can conclude that any cat being talked about is a purple one.

Words and grammatical rules are the basic building blocks that allow us to encode and decode meanings in language. Once we know them, we can handle novel sentences perfectly smoothly when they crop up in the course of a text or conversation, with no breakdown in communication. Being proficient in a language involves the (initially puzzling) ability to handle all sorts of new combinations of its words. The puzzle is solved if we think of language as generating new meaningful combinations of words (being 'productive') and doing so because it contains a system of rules for combining and recombining those basic building blocks (being 'systematic').

In sum, despite the fact that humans—like other animals—have only a finite capacity to commit vocabulary to memory, our languages allow meanings to be encoded and decoded in potentially limitless ways. So, while there are some similarities between human languages and non-human animal languages (e.g. in allowing their users to indicate aspects of their environment) there are also significant differences, including a huge step-change in expressive power.

Contemplating the important creative possibilities of language brings us to a constraint on a theory of meaning in language: it must specify the mechanisms by which a potentially infinite number of complex meanings can be generated from a finite base. A huge amount of detailed work is involved in carefully analysing the properties of all of the expressions and rules of human languages which make this possible. This work is undertaken primarily by linguists and is crucial for understanding why, and how, linguistic utterances mean what they do.

Meaning and practice

Meaning in language depends on the practices of those who use it, with human powers of imagination and lateral thinking colouring our communication. We often express meanings that are indirect, metaphorical, playful, or surreptitious. Sometimes these follow broad patterns. Imagine, for example, that I am looking out of the window at the pouring rain. I say to you, 'What a lovely day,' in a deeply ironic tone. In doing so, I manage to convey something—namely, that I think it is a *horrible* day. Yet this is precisely the opposite of what my words actually mean. In many instances like this one, we need to draw a distinction between what words mean—strictly speaking—and what we use them to communicate on any particular occasion.

We looked at a particularly urgent example of this phenomenon at the start of this chapter, asking whether an utterance of 'Let him have it' should be understood as expressing a kind of literal meaning (something like *Let the policeman have the gun*) or whether the speaker should be understood more colloquially (as communicating *Shoot the policeman*), but the potential divergence between what words mean, strictly speaking, and what we can use them to communicate is endemic in our linguistic practice. For instance, another sort of example emerges from the following dialogue:

ALICE: Do you think Charlie cheated on the exam?
BISHMA: Well, it would be fairly miraculous to get top marks without doing any work whatsoever.

Bishma does not explicitly voice the opinion that Charlie cheated. Nevertheless, by choosing to answer Alice's question in such a way, he strongly suggests that Charlie must have cheated. Again, what is communicated seems to diverge from what the words strictly and literally mean.

Examples of irony and insinuation illustrate in a couple of different ways the distinction between what we will call 'standing meaning' and 'speaker meaning'. Standing meaning captures the conventional meaning of a word or sentence in a given language. Meanwhile, speaker meaning picks out what a word or sentence is used to convey on a particular occasion of use. Ultimately, an account of meaning will need to say something about both speaker meaning and standing meaning, and how the two are related. Or, to put the issue another way, we will need to try and answer the question, 'How do we know what someone means by what they say?'

The distinction between standing meaning and speaker meaning is often cast as a difference between 'semantics' and 'pragmatics'. There is a lively debate in linguistics and the philosophy of language about exactly how to define and separate these categories of meaning (and indeed, theorists argue about whether they can ultimately be separated at all). As we saw earlier, 'semantics' is often used as a general label for the contents of our words, relating to our mindful engagement with things in the world. Yet in many discussions of the semantics–pragmatics distinction, 'semantics' is used more narrowly, to capture the standing, conventional meanings of simple and complex expressions, rather than the full contents they convey on particular occasions of use. Pragmatics, in contrast, concerns the meanings that get produced on the fly, where the contribution of particular expressions can vary wildly across contexts. Again, our exploration of meaning will need to say something about these different elements of language and communication, with the aim of providing a clearer picture of how our words channel meaning.

By this point, we have already identified a small wish list for any account of meaning in language:

- Explain what meaning is and where meaning in language comes from.
- Explain how the meanings of complex expressions, like sentences, are built up from simpler parts, like words, according to a finite set of rules.
- Explain how the standing meanings of words and sentences relate to the meanings that speakers communicate.

As we will see in future chapters, some of these objectives pull in opposite directions. For example, the requirement that complex meanings be built up from simpler parts according to a finite set of rules suggests a picture of linguistic communication as something which is logical, conventional, and predictable. In contrast, the need to account for speaker meaning and pragmatics calls for a more complex and contextually nuanced picture, which appeals to all sorts of wider understandings, associations, and imaginative leaps. It turns out that finding the right balance between these two opposing pictures constitutes a major challenge for those seeking to understand meaning.

Chapter 2
Meaning and practical problems

Meaning is a complex, fascinating, and important phenomenon and it is certainly worth exploring just for its own sake. Beyond this, however, a further reason to want a theory of meaning is because having such an account might help us solve certain puzzles or practical problems. For instance, if we know what underpins word meaning in human languages we will be better placed to answer vexed questions about meaning in other systems (like whether the artificially produced utterances of AI systems are meaningful, or whether the signs of an animal language have meaning) or to be able to explain what underpins the ability of human infants to acquire their first language. Furthermore, having an account of meaning in language will allow us to better understand what is going on in specific kinds of real-world discourse or with particular kinds of expression.

In recent years, much academic work in this area has taken something of an 'applied turn', with theorists wondering about issues such as how to draw the distinction between lying and misleading, how to think about the meaning of slurs and other offensive expressions, and how these expressions should be regulated, for example by 'hate speech' laws. Looking at some of the practical issues which have exercised theorists in this area will allow us to see how abstract questions about meaning are fundamentally connected with pressing topics in contemporary life.

Lying and misleading

Intuitively, it might seem easy to define what a lie is: a speaker lies if they say something they know (or believe) to be false, with the intention of deceiving their audience. In fact, however, all aspects of this simple definition have been questioned by philosophers. From our current point of view, one important point to note is that, if we are to use this kind of definition to work out when someone is lying, we will need to have a firm grip on what it is for someone to say something false. Yet this turns out to be a pretty fraught issue.

To see the problem here, consider this case (which follows one discussed by the philosopher Jennifer Saul): imagine that an ageing relative, from whom I've been distanced for many years, is planning on leaving me some money in her will, but only if she thinks that I have lived my life fully in line with Christian teaching. I would like to receive the money but know that if my relative realizes I had my children out of wedlock she will not make the bequest. Given these facts, it seems that I might decide to utter the sentence,

'I got married and had two children.'

I fully expect that my utterance will lead my relative to believe that I got married and *then* had children, so I am intentionally trying to mislead her. Yet, if challenged, intuitively it seems I could resist the claim that I *lied* (so long as it's true that I got married and it's true that I had children, even if not in that order). This intuitive defence, however, rests on a particular understanding of the meaning of the connective term 'and'—specifically, I didn't lie if 'and' means just the conjunction of two claims.

On the other hand, if 'and', on at least some occasions, can have a richer meaning, akin to 'and *then*', what I literally said is false. For, if 'and' has this richer meaning, then what I explicitly assert in this context is that *I got married and then had two children*, a claim we are supposing I know to be false. On this second analysis of the meaning of 'and', I can rightly be charged with lying, that is, to be saying something that I know to be false with the intention of deceiving my audience.

It might seem, at first blush, that this difference is not terribly important, for it is not clear from the toy case above that very much turns on the distinction between lying and misleading. Whether I inherit the money, for instance, turns only on whether my relative believes that I got married and then had children; it doesn't matter whether she forms that belief because I successfully misled her or successfully lied to her. Yet in many other situations, the distinction really does matter.

For instance, the legal offence of perjury (lying under oath) carries significant penalties in most legal jurisdictions, while misleading under oath is not similarly penalized. To apply the legal notion of perjury, however, requires us to draw a distinction between lying as opposed to misleading. Furthermore, it seems that the legal frameworks reflect the social or cultural fact that there is something special about lying, with the speaker who lies opening themselves up (in most situations—'white lies' being a probable exception) to a special kind of moral opprobrium or censure. Again, however, we can only make sense of this kind of special moral offence if we know what it is to tell a lie and, as we have seen, that is going to depend on knowing which meaning someone is committed to, and in what way, by the words and sentences they produce.

Toxic speech

Another area where understanding meaning in language matters, and one which has received an increasing level of interest in academic circles in recent years, concerns speech seen as unpleasant, offensive, or oppressive. A central case study is that of pejorative expressions or slurs—offensive terms used to target, and show a lack of respect for, a particular group or class of people (often defined by race, gender, or religion).

Discussing these expressions in academic work is notoriously difficult, for it seems that the terms retain their capacity to shock and offend even when (as philosophers put it) they are being mentioned, or attributed to someone else, rather than actually being used by the speaker themselves. That is to say, pejorative terms have the power to offend even when they are 'marked off' in some way. For instance, in 'Mary said that Isa was a lesbian' it is clear that the speaker is attributing the statement to Mary. In this kind of 'indirect discourse' context, a speaker is not committed to endorsing the claim being attributed; in our example sentence, the speaker doesn't commit to the truth of Isa being a lesbian, they merely note that that is what Mary claimed. Consider, in contrast, 'Mary said that Isa was a d***.' In this case it seems that the speaker shares culpability with Mary for the slur. Even though its use is being attributed to Mary, the pejorative term retains its offensive power. Indeed, there is a risk that the culpability extends further, so that even reproducing the expression as an example of pejorative language carries the risk of offence (hence we used stars rather than articulating the slur in full).

Clearly, then, enclosing pejorative terms within indirect discourse, embedded quotation, or other linguistic devices does not (or at least, not always) serve to divorce a speaker from the negative connotations associated with uses of the term. This persistence in the power to offend has been held by many to indicate that the problem lies in the meanings of the terms themselves, that is, within the standing meaning or semantic content of these expressions, which differs from that of their neutral counterparts (so it is held that the words 'lesbian' and 'd***' have different literal meanings).

Although there are reasons to think that pejorative terms have meanings which differ from their neutral counterparts, there are also problems with this approach. For instance, while it is true that very often pejorative terms retain their power to offend, there is also the phenomenon of 'reclamation' to account for. A group which has been the target of a pejorative term may, under certain conditions, reclaim the term and use it to refer to themselves in a positive way.

The conditions of reclamation are difficult to state, but seem at least to require that a majority of the target group, or the subset of the group which reclaims the term, are willing to countenance a non-offensive in-group usage. Reclamation is delicate, for it usually involves acceptable in-group uses while the term retains its pejorative status when used by out-group members, or if it is used outside certain kinds of limited conversational domains. However, the mere fact that at least *sometimes* a pejorative term can have acceptable uses (apparently *without* coming to have two distinct meanings—a pejorative and a neutral one) seems to undermine the claim that the power to offend is located directly within the meaning of the expression itself.

Concerns about semantic approaches have led some people to suggest alternative analyses of pejorative expressions, such as treating the offensive element as part of the contextual meaning, or pragmatic content, of the term. For instance, it has been suggested that the offensive content of a pejorative term might form part of what is indirectly conveyed by speakers using the term. Alternatively, we might think that the pejorative aspect of these terms lies in the constraints that exist on their appropriate contexts of use (roughly, for example, that 'd***' can only be used appropriately if one holds offensive views about lesbians or if one belongs to a group which has successfully reclaimed this term for non-offensive use).

Obviously, we can't hope to settle the debate about the meaning of pejorative terms here, but we can see why the debate matters.

Getting clear on where the harm lies in pejorative language helps us to see how to proceed with these kinds of expressions. For instance, if the offensive element is part of the term's semantic meaning, then we should either exclude the term altogether or find a way to change its meaning. On the other hand, if the offence arises through pragmatic, contextual features, it seems we might seek to reclaim a slurring term but to alter its pragmatic associations. Studying the meaning of slurs can help to clarify the concepts and beliefs behind pejorative language, revealing how we ought to mitigate the harmfulness of such charged language. In this way, theories which clarify the meaning of pejorative terms could be used to create change, finding a place within activist movements in this area.

Philosophers including Jason Stanley, Justin Khoo, and Jennifer Saul have argued that many of the words we use in political and social discourse share crucial features with slurs. Words that are, at first blush, much less likely to cause immediate offence (like 'welfare' or 'migrant crisis') may nevertheless carry pejorative content. So, describing someone as 'on welfare' may explicitly assert only that they are in receipt of government assistance, whilst covertly conveying discriminatory claims about those who fall into this group (such as that those in receipt of welfare are lazy or undeserving). According to these analyses of so-called 'code words' or 'dogwhistles', the associations will linger—even a politician who is arguing that welfare rates should be increased, or that welfare should be extended to a previously excluded group, may be unable to avoid indirectly communicating pejorative content.

Such analyses point to one way in which discriminatory ideologies can gain traction, by hijacking our language and the meanings we can express. If they are right (and we should note that the claims are controversial), the language used in democracies (no less than that used in dictatorships) turns out to contribute to the perpetuating and entrenching of ideas in subtle and complex ways, and thus to serve as a form of political propaganda.

The philosopher Lynn Tirrell has proposed that propaganda operates through networks of ideas connected to the uses of expressions. For instance, Tirrell examines how descriptions of the Rwandan Tutsi population as 'inzoka' (meaning *snakes*) or 'inyenzi' (meaning *cockroaches*) facilitated the subsequent genocide (and even the specific ways in which people were killed), by licensing lethal actions normally considered appropriate for snakes or cockroaches. Making a more general point, Tirrell identifies a wide-ranging category of 'toxic speech' which serves to normalize various problematic thoughts and behaviours by bringing to salience a network of problematic ideas in the minds of language users.

Within the broad category of toxic speech, hate speech has been an area of particular interest to philosophers. On the one hand, this is because the topic raises issues in political philosophy concerning the balance between regulating harmful speech and preserving the right to free expression. On the other, it is of interest to philosophers of language because of the difficulties involved in defining and identifying hate speech.

Theorists have sought to make progress on questions of definition and identification by exploring whether hate speech is a matter of the speaker's intentions, the meanings of the words used, or wider social contexts (such as whether the target social group is the subject of structural injustice). They have also investigated whether the term 'hate speech' itself has a unified meaning across legal and ordinary discourse, and what the implications are for the law if the way in which ordinary speakers understand the term does not fully coincide with the way in which it is understood in legal contexts. The conclusions drawn in these philosophical discussions about the meaning of 'hate speech' clearly have real-world implications for the development of legal, regulatory, and wider social practices.

Another domain in which questions of meaning have come to the forefront as having potentially serious practical repercussions emerges from feminist philosophy. Philosophers like Jennifer Hornsby and Rae Langton have used theoretical claims about speech acts to explain why pornography should be considered as damaging. For instance, Langton argues that pornography should be construed as subordinating and silencing women, limiting their ability to refuse sexual intercourse. When a woman says 'no' to sex she intends to refuse to have sex, but pornography, Langton suggests, increases the likelihood that she goes unheard (either because she is heard as refusing but is nevertheless forced to have sex, or because she is not even heard as refusing). This kind of approach, which uses tools developed within philosophy of language to contribute to debates surrounding gender equality issues, provides another example of the way in which discussions about meaning, and about how we communicate what we mean to others, can turn out to be relevant to fundamental societal issues.

Understanding harmful speech has become an increasingly urgent task as the scale and speed of online communication has exploded. Social media platforms host vast amounts of speech, disseminated to enormous numbers of users on a second-by-second basis. Inevitably, some of this content is liable to cause harm, be it by inciting terrorist acts, hate crimes, or other forms of violence, or by promoting self-harm or suicide, or by spreading misinformation that damages people's abilities to make good judgements. As platforms and regulators try to get to grips with these problems, content moderation has become a core feature of the online sphere, with users' speech sometimes being blocked, removed, labelled, or otherwise 'de-amplified' (meaning that fewer users see it in their feeds).

Yet the question of how to make content moderation decisions— especially at such large scales—is a vexed one. While it would be possible to ban particular words or phrases, context often plays a crucial role in determining what is really being meant or communicated with them. For example, a potentially violating phrase might be used merely ironically or rhetorically. Perhaps it is even being deployed in an attempt to counter another's hateful speech, and should be encouraged rather than quashed. In practice, then, online platforms must attempt to deliver contextually nuanced judgements through the policies being enforced by teams of human moderators and, increasingly, machine algorithms. Questions about the facts underpinning meaning in language will be at the heart of these judgements.

Meaning and the law

One area in which claims about meaning in language are particularly pertinent comes from consideration of legal practices. For instance, a key canon of interpretation in many legal frameworks is the 'ordinary meaning' requirement, whereby words are to be understood in their ordinary, everyday sense unless the context indicates that they have a special, technical sense (in the UK, this is captured in the 'Plain Meaning Rule' of statutory interpretation).

That words in legal (and governmental) statements should, in general, come with their ordinary meanings attached is important since the idea of fair notice is a cornerstone of our democratic system (that is to say, legal requirements imposed by the state on citizens must be accessible to, and comprehensible by, those who are to be governed by the laws, i.e. citizens must be given fair notice of the demands placed on them). However, unless the laws of the land are written in terms ordinary people can understand, this requirement for fair notice is not likely to be met. Ensuring legal terms are generally interpreted in a way that preserves their ordinary meaning thus matters.

The focus on the role that ordinary meaning plays in the law has given rise to a highly influential, but also very controversial, school of thought concerning the meaning of legal writing known as 'textualism'. According to textualism, legal texts should be interpreted by paying attention to their ordinary meaning (as opposed to, say, interpreting the law by thinking about what legislators might have intended or reflecting on the purpose the law is supposed to serve). Famous advocates of textualism, like Antonin Scalia (a conservative judge who sat on the Supreme Court of the United States from 1986 until 2016), have used textualism to argue against interpretations which they claim alter or update the meaning of legal terms. For instance, Scalia argued that the phrase 'the right of the people to keep and bear arms' in the US constitution must be understood as enshrining the right of an *individual* to carry weapons, as this was how the expression 'bear arms' was commonly understood at the time the constitution was written (a claim that has been queried by those working on the historical understanding of language).

Textualism rests on the assumption that there is a clear (and unique) ordinary meaning to be discovered for most terms, but this assumption is one that we might query. For instance, in a now classic example, the famous legal theorist H. L. A. Hart raised the following question: 'A legal rule forbids you to take a vehicle into the public park. Plainly this forbids an automobile, but what about bicycles, roller skates, toy automobiles? What about airplanes? Are these, as we say, to be called "vehicles" for the purpose of the rule or not?' As Hart's example shows, when we come to apply legal rules we apparently find that their meaning is not determinate enough to settle all the cases that may arise (Figure 4).

Furthermore, Hart's worry is not just an abstract 'thought experiment', as can be seen from an actual case discussed at length by the philosopher Stephen Neale: US statute 18 U.S.C. § 924(c)(1) mandates a five-year consecutive sentence for anyone who 'uses or carries a firearm during and in relation to any crime of violence or drug trafficking'. In *Smith v. United States* (1993), a defendant appealed the application of this penalty in his own case as he had attempted to trade a firearm for drugs rather than using the gun in a more conventional sense. The defendant eventually lost his appeal, with the Supreme Court finding that his actions *did*

4. H. L. A. Hart's famous example of a park sign, raising questions about what counts as a 'vehicle'.

constitute the use of a firearm in relation to a crime of drug trafficking.

The Supreme Court here adopted a *very* general understanding of the meaning of 'use', whereby the term could correctly apply to pretty much any form of interaction between the agent and the gun. Of course, not everyone agreed with this finding, with opponents arguing that the expression should have been interpreted in this context using a much richer, much less general meaning, such as 'used in a threatening fashion' or 'used in the sense typical for a gun'. Yet whichever interpretation you think is right here, the disagreement is clearly a dispute about the proper meaning of the term 'use'.

Appreciation of this problem has led to an increased interest recently in empirical methods that might help to isolate the ordinary meaning of difficult or contested terms. So, for instance, legal theorists and other practitioners have suggested it might be possible to create questionnaires or surveys, to be taken by the general public, which might help to draw out the consensus view on what the ordinary meaning of some term is (e.g. people might be presented with various short vignettes or descriptions which make use of the term 'vehicle' and be asked whether the use of the term in that context is appropriate or not). Such methods, however, are time-consuming and costly and are unlikely to be practicable in most cases.

Alternatively (or in addition), then, there has been growing interest in what 'big data' approaches might contribute to legal interpretation. These approaches rely on so-called 'Corpus Linguistics', a branch of linguistics that involves the study of large datasets of digitized texts (the 'corpus') and the use of specialized software capable of analysing the statistical properties of items in the corpus. One common form of analysis involves spotting 'collocations', that is, words which appear together in a corpus with a frequency greater than chance (as noted in Chapter 1, this property is important in the generation of language strings by so-called 'Large Language Models', like OpenAI's ChatGPT and Google's Gemini systems).

Corpus linguistics has been used to query the suggestion (attributed above to Judge Scalia, though he is certainly not the only one to make it) that the phrase 'the right of the people to keep and bear arms' in the US constitution must be understood as expressing the right of *individuals* to keep and carry weapons. Studies of corpora created from US writings concurrent with the constitution reveal that the phrase actually co-occurs much more commonly with terms referring to militia and armies than individuals.

While the extent to which empirical approaches (like corpus linguistics, questionnaires, and surveys) can really settle questions of legal interpretation remains a matter of debate, there is no doubt that they provide an interesting and innovative approach to the question of how to discover the ordinary meaning of words and phrases. Furthermore, as the *Smith v. United States* case makes clear, settling questions of meaning can have the most serious import for people's lives.

Reasoning and interpretation

Finally, questions of meaning in language have also recently come to the fore in debates about the nature of human thinking, and the extent to which we can be considered good, logical reasoners versus thinkers who fall prey to biases and illogicality. An excellent example of this debate emerges from so-called 'framing effects'.

'Framing effects' arise when people's decisions are influenced by the way in which options are presented to them, without any substantial change to the options themselves. For instance, in experiments, people have been shown to prefer a basketball player who is described as having 'made 80% of their shots' over one who is described as having 'missed 20% of their shots' (so, in a hypothetical situation where participants are asked to construct a basketball team, they will be willing to pay more for players described in the first way over those described in the second). Yet, logically, these two claims seem identical—to make 80 per cent of one's shots *just is* to miss 20 per cent.

This finding has been used (most famously by psychologists Daniel Kahneman and Amos Tversky) to argue that people are standardly pretty poor decision makers. Instead of arriving at decisions through the operation of logical rules and statistical reasoning, we allow ourselves to be blown this way and that by apparently irrelevant features of the choices we face (such as whether the options are being described in positive or negative terms).

On reflection, however, questions of meaning are clearly relevant here and may, in fact, show that framing cases do not reveal the weakness of human thinking. For *what a speaker means* can diverge from what the words and sentences the speaker produces literally mean (the classic example involves someone uttering 'It is a lovely day' but conveying that *it is a horrible day*). Appealing to this idea of speaker meaning may be relevant here, for it seems that the mere fact that a speaker chooses a positive over a negative frame of reference (or vice versa) may itself be informative, allowing the speaker to (indirectly) communicate something potentially important by her choice.

Describing a player as 'making 80% of their shots' might be thought to pragmatically convey something positive to the audience (along the lines of *80 per cent is a good percentage of shots to make*), while describing a player as 'missing 20 per cent of their shots' conveys something negative (along the lines of *20 per cent is a lot of shots to miss*). Sensitivity to speaker meaning and to the pragmatic dimensions of communication could explain why people's preferences shift in framing cases *without* any sort of appeal to irrationality. Perhaps, then, instead of showing that we are systematically poor thinkers, framing cases instead reveal just how capable and accomplished we are when it comes to questions of meaning in language.

Understanding meaning in language and beyond

The examples looked at in this chapter illustrate some of the practical implications that follow from decisions about the meanings of words and sentences. Only if we know what particular words mean—and what speakers are able to convey by uttering those words in specific contexts—can we work out whether someone is lying or merely misleading, whether slurs and other offensive terms should be expunged from the language or can be reclaimed, how best to combat propaganda and the insidious ideas that pejorative terms encourage, and how to settle debates about contested terms in the law in a principled and consistent way. Questions about the meanings carried by linguistic signs, then, clearly matter.

So how might we try to answer these questions? In the rest of this book we want to explore three different approaches to the way in which signs become meaningful: through their connection with things in the world (Chapters 3 and 4), through their connection with thoughts and minds (Chapters 5 and 6), and through the way they are used (Chapter 7). In order to make things more concrete we will continue to focus our attention on the question of how linguistic signs (words, sentences, and utterances) become meaningful, but it seems clear that these three sources are also the main contenders for grounding meaning in general. For instance, what makes a painting or picture meaningful might be that it represents features of the world, or that it was intended by the painter to have a certain meaning (or is believed to have a given meaning by viewers), or that the picture plays a part in a certain kind of practice (e.g. being used to warn drivers that old people may be crossing the road here). Indeed, even for the most abstract, deep, and difficult questions about meaning, such as 'what is the meaning of life?', a case can be made that these three factors will be relevant. Perhaps a meaningful life is one which seeks discoveries about, or is properly embedded in, the external and social world, or one which the subject herself thinks has value, or one that fulfils a certain kind of purpose or role. So, when thinking about meaning in any sphere, it will be useful to keep these three sources in mind and ask which one is doing the work in grounding claims about meaning.

Chapter 3
Meaning and objects

To resolve the sort of practical problems explored in the last chapter we need to be able to answer a fundamental theoretical question: 'What makes any linguistic sign meaningful?' (or, in more general terms, when we are not restricting our attention to words and utterances, 'Where does meaning come from?'). Recall our discussion of slurring terms in Chapter 2 and the practical question of whether an offensive expression should simply be banned (e.g. on social media platforms) or whether, instead, context should be taken to be relevant (allowing for the possibility that some uses of the term might be non-offensive). To resolve this practical question, we need to know *what* the meaning of the target term is, and that requires knowing, in turn, *which features* are relevant for determining meaning. We are now in a position to introduce our first substantive answer. According to this first view, *the meaning of a sign is given by the thing(s) in the world which it picks out*.

The intuitive force behind this idea—which we will call the *referential* approach to meaning—is easy to see. Take a toy example: imagine that I've got a new puppy and decide to name it 'Walker'. I tell my friends and family that that is the puppy's name and I go to the shop and buy a collar and tag, engraved with the name, and hang that around the dog's neck. This instance of the name 'Walker' now refers to this puppy and it can be used by you and others in our linguistic community to talk about this particular dog (as in 'Walker has eaten my slippers again!'). It seems that the name here is nothing more than a simple label for the object and what makes the expression meaningful is just its role in picking out, and allowing us to talk about, this particular thing in the world. Or again, consider someone who is learning a foreign language, or a child acquiring their first natural language: it would seem reasonable for a teacher to start by demonstrating the connection between the simple signs of the language and what they signify, for example holding up a ball and saying 'This is called "la balle" in French' or 'This is a *ball*.'

The idea that the meaning of a sign depends on the thing in the world that it picks out has a long history, and it has been used to provide both an account of the meaning of specific types of linguistic expression and as a general model of meaning (encompassing all sorts of signs).

The meaning of names

In philosophy, one of the most famous referential accounts of the meaning of a specific kind of expression belongs to the 19th-century English thinker John Stuart Mill. Mill held that there is a particular category of words—proper names—whose meaning is given entirely through their connection to things in the world. A genuine name, according to Mill, does not describe an object in any way, nor does it attach to its referent because of any property the object possesses, rather a name is an 'unmeaning mark' which we arbitrarily stick on an object for communicative ease.

Returning to our toy example of the name 'Walker': say you discover that my new pet isn't in fact a dog at all (perhaps I've actually bought a wolf cub), or perhaps you find out that I'm just pretending he's mine when really he belongs to my neighbour.

Clearly, you've made a mistake about the properties the new pet has. Still these mistakes don't seem to affect to whom or what the name refers. A speaker who says 'Walker ate my slippers' says something about that particular biting, snarling animal with the 'Walker' name tag round its neck, even if that animal isn't a dog, has a different owner to the one you originally thought, and so on.

Mill's own example of this point concerned the name 'Dartmouth'. If there were a descriptive property associated with that name, it seems reasonable to think it would be 'the town at the mouth of the River Dart'. Yet as Mill noted, if the river changed course, so that some other city came to be located at its mouth, that other city wouldn't automatically inherit the name 'Dartmouth'. Dartmouth, it seems, remains 'Dartmouth' regardless of whether it is actually situated at the mouth of the River Dart or not (and the same goes for the town's other properties). According to Mill, then, a name is nothing more than an ad hoc label for an object; and its meaning is completely given by the thing in the world to which it attaches.

This Millian approach to names has been widely adopted. For instance, a number of contemporary theories in linguistics assume that there are fundamental elements in a language whose function is simply to stand for objects. One reason for this uptake is that the approach apparently provides a very concrete, unmysterious account of what meaning is. If we take meaning to lie in the fact that a linguistic expression (or any other kind of sign) is connected to some aspect of, or object in, the world, we reduce the abstract and difficult notion of meaning to something much more tractable. From a philosophical point of view, the approach promises to 'make meaning naturalistically respectable', that is, to show how meaning fits within our ordinary, scientific understanding of the world. This appealing feature has led some theorists to seek ways in which the referential approach can be broadened out from a concentration on just proper names.

Extending the referential model

One way to extend Mill's approach would be to apply it to other types of linguistic expressions. So, for instance, consider expressions like 'this dog', 'that cat', 'I', 'you', 'here', and 'tomorrow' (philosophers call expressions like the first pair on this list *demonstratives* and ones like the last four *indexicals*). All of these expressions seem to behave in a way very similar to names—they select objects in the world and they seem to be indifferent to the properties people think those objects possess. So, take the expressions 'I' and 'now'. It seems that an utterance of 'I' picks out as the referent whoever produces it and 'now' picks out the time of utterance, regardless of any further properties possessed by the speaker or the time. My audience and I may firmly believe that I am Margaret Thatcher and that the date today is 28 November 1990, but if I now say 'I'm leaving government today' I say something (false) about *myself at the time of utterance*, and not something (true) about Thatcher in November 1990. Like names, then, these expressions seem to refer to things in a way that is independent of the properties speakers or hearers take those objects to have. This has led some philosophers of language to argue that they are 'directly referential'—although the expressions come with a rule of use (e.g. 'I' has something like the rule of use 'pick out the person who has uttered the word "I"'), once they are used they acquire their meaning directly from the things in the world to which they attach, just as proper names do.

Getting the meaning of demonstrative and indexical expressions right matters, for it seems these expressions mark an important (and, some philosophers have argued, irreducibly special) way of thinking about objects in the world, a way which influences how we act. To see this, consider the following thought experiment (borrowed from the philosopher John Perry): imagine that you are in a supermarket doing your shopping when you notice a trail of sugar on the ground. You think to yourself, 'Oh, there is a shopper who has a leaky bag of sugar in their trolley.' In an effort to warn them of this, you follow the trail of sugar around the aisles, until eventually it leads you right back to where you started, whereupon you exclaim, 'My goodness, *I* have the leaky sugar bag!' (Note the same point holds if we imagine that you are merely accompanying the shopper who has the leaky bag; what is required then is the realization 'Oh. *You* have the leaky bag.')

The question Perry posed was what changes between thinking that *there is a shopper with a leaky bag* and thinking an indexical thought like *I have a leaky bag* or *You have a leaky bag*. Both the description 'a shopper with a leaky bag' and the indexical expression ('I' or 'you'), in this context, pick out one and the same person. Yet it is only when you think about that person in the special way indicated by an expression like 'I' or 'you' that you are able to take appropriate action to stop the leak. It seems that being told more descriptive information (e.g. that the shopper with the leaky bag has a red jumper on, is female, has blonde hair, is 170 cm tall, etc.) might not help here, for you could always fail to realize that it is *you* that fits the description. What is needed instead is a shift from purely descriptive claims to the special kind of direct reference encoded by expressions like 'I' and 'you'.

So, some kind of referential model of meaning seems attractive for names and for some other kinds of expressions, like 'I', 'you', 'this', or 'that'. However, it becomes harder to see what things in the world might be available to provide the meanings of other kinds of words. For instance, we need an account of meaning for expressions like verbs and adjectives, but there are no objects (on a par with people and pets) for these expressions to refer to. This isn't to say that the referential picture *can't* be applied in these cases, but to note that the move to locate meaning in worldly reference may not be equally intuitive for all expressions.

An alternative way to generalize the referential model would be to use it as an account of the meaning of *all* signs and symbols, not merely linguistic ones. One philosopher who adopts the referential perspective in this way is Ruth Millikan. Millikan holds that it is our shared practice of giving and receiving information about external states of affairs that makes language meaningful. (Her approach thus looks to two sources for meaning: appealing to the world—to underpin the idea of language as a system for conveying information—and to our practices—a source of meaning we will focus on in Chapter 6.) So, for instance, the English word 'dog' means what it does because speakers use it for communicating information about dogs, and hearers think about dogs when they hear the word. Without this role in conveying information about the world, 'dog' would no longer mean *dog* in English, and without any kind of role in conveying information, the expression would no longer mean anything at all. The model here holds, Millikan claims, not just for expressions in natural language but for any other kind of sign or symbol.

For instance, consider 'natural signs', like foot- or paw-prints. Imagine that people come to realize that a particular set of tracks in a snowy forest reveals the presence of partridges. Then, because those kinds of tracks can be used as reliable indicators of partridges, we can say that those tracks mean *partridge*, that is, they carry the information that a certain kind of bird is present in the local environment. Millikan labels the role that a sign plays in carrying information about the external world its 'proper function' and she notes that proper functions are tied to domains, that is, to parts of the world where the signs perform the function in question. To see this, consider another forest, where there are both partridges and pheasants and where these birds make tracks which viewers happen to find indistinguishable. Relative to this forest, the very same set of tracks will no longer be reliable indicators of partridges for a viewer. However, they could be used as a reliable indicator of a larger set, namely the set of [pheasants or partridges]. Relative to this second forest, then, we can say that the tracks in the snow mean [*pheasant or partridge*], even though relative to the first forest an instance of the very same track marks simply means *partridge*. And as for tracks in the snow, so for any other kind of meaningful sign. What makes a sign meaningful is that it has a purpose, realized by pairs of sign producers and consumers, to convey information; and that uses of the sign now occur due to the precedent set by past uses.

Finally, instead of (or in addition to) using the referential approach to analyse the meaning of names, other linguistic expressions, or signs more generally, we could decide to treat the referential model as giving a quite general account of the role or function of language. This move seems quite plausible because language plays a pivotal role in allowing us to acquire and transmit information about our environment. Think about all the things you know about the world around you. While some of this information will have been acquired through perception (e.g. you know it's raining because you can see the wet pavement or hear the raindrops hitting the window), a huge swathe of the things you know in fact come from what others have told you.

The *testimony* other people provide gives us a way to find out about things we haven't, or can't, experience directly for ourselves: I know that you had soup for lunch because you tell me so; I believe that the sun is around 93 million miles away from the Earth because I read this in a book written by an expert. Some theorists have suggested, then, that we should think about language, just like perception, as providing a route for acquiring knowledge about the external world. In this way, we can approach linguistic meaning in general in terms of the information linguistic claims convey. In the next chapter, we look in detail at how this kind of referential approach to the function of language and to issues of meaning might be pursued.

The referential approach, then, has been highly influential in the study of meaning, both as an account of the meaning of some set of linguistic expressions and as an all-encompassing model of the meaning of signs. However, despite its attractions (e.g. in terms of simplicity and showing how meaning fits into the natural world), it is not without its problems.

Problems with the referential model of word meaning

There are (at least) three serious objections to the idea that the meaning of a name can be given by the thing in the world to which it refers. First, some names have more than one referent. Second, some names have no referent at all. Third, sometimes the meaning of a name involves more than just its referent. Let's take these in turn.

First, many readers will have spotted that our discussion of names above made a pretty fundamental simplifying assumption: namely, that words and objects map 1–1, with each name having exactly one referent. But of course, that's not right. 'Aristotle' was the name of an ancient Greek philosopher, but also of a 20th-century Greek shipping magnate, and of many other individuals besides. So, it would be a mistake simply to say that the name 'Aristotle' refers to the Greek philosopher. In answer to the recognition that proper names can have multiple referents, one suggestion is that we should individuate names more finely. Instead of saying that there is one name 'Aristotle' which has its meaning given by the person to whom it refers, we should posit lots of different names which just happen to look and sound the same. According to this line of argument, what we really have is a set of different names, 'Aristotle$_1$', 'Aristotle$_2$', etc., with the referent of each being fixed by causal and historical facts about the name's lineage.

This kind of view has been defended by the philosopher Saul Kripke. According to Kripke, one instance of the name 'Aristotle', call it 'Aristotle$_1$', refers to the Greek philosopher because there was an initial 'baptism' where the name got associated with that particular individual (crudely, someone who was in direct contact with that particular individual announced that that individual would have this name). My use of the name 'Aristotle$_1$' now shares that same reference because it belongs to a chain of uses which can in principle be traced all the way back to that initial naming ceremony.

Meanwhile, there is another (superficially identical) name 'Aristotle$_2$' which refers to a Greek shipping magnate, again because it belongs to a historical chain of uses tracing back to an original act of naming, which connected that term to that individual. While this kind of causal-historical theory of the meaning of names is itself open to challenge, it does provide at least a possible answer to the objection that names can have multiple name referents, without giving up on the idea that the meaning of a name is given by the thing in the world to which it refers. However, our other two challenges to the referential approach seem more serious.

Whereas our initial challenge concerned cases where there were *too many* potential referents, our second challenge concerns cases where there are *not enough* potential referents—so-called 'empty names'. One rich source of empty names comes from fiction. Take a name like 'Sherlock Holmes': despite the number of letters that the Post Office report as sent to 221B Baker St each year, Sherlock Holmes never actually existed. There is thus no object in the world available to provide the name's meaning. Yet we certainly don't want to conclude that names like 'Sherlock' or 'Pegasus' are meaningless.

One possible response to this worry would be to liberalize the things we will count as objects of reference, accepting fictional objects as referents (alongside real-world objects, like dogs and cats and philosophers). This sort of approach was recommended by 19th-century Austrian philosopher and psychologist Alexius Meinong. Meinong held that the things we include in our list of the contents of the world shouldn't be limited to things which actually exist. Instead, non-existent objects should also be countenanced.

However, a move like this would seem to undermine one of the key motivations we had for adopting a referential model in the first place, namely that it holds out the promise of a non-mysterious, scientifically respectable account of meaning. Fictional objects are not scientifically respectable, so if we treat them as potential objects of reference we undermine the naturalistic credentials of the approach.

An alternative response to the worry about empty names, then, and one which has seemed appealing to many theorists, is to deny J. S. Mill's assumption that the meaning of a name is exhausted by the object to which it refers. This brings us to our third challenge: that the meaning of a name sometimes involves more than just its referent. Perhaps instead of, or alongside, an external object, the meaning of a name should be viewed as containing some descriptive content, as telling us something about how the referent is viewed or thought about. For instance, perhaps the name 'Aristotle$_1$' is associated with a property like 'the greatest Ancient Greek philosopher' or 'the teacher of Alexander', etc. So, when someone uses this term, perhaps to say, 'Aristotle wrote the *Nicomachean Ethics,*' what they express is a claim like *the Ancient Greek philosopher who taught Alexander the Great wrote the Nicomachean Ethics.*

This kind of approach would be particularly helpful when we think about empty or fictional names, for we could say that although such expressions lack a referent they are not meaningless—they still convey a descriptive content. For example, perhaps the name 'Sherlock Holmes' is associated with a description like 'the fictional detective, created by Sir Arthur Conan Doyle, who was said to live at 221B Baker St, London', while 'Pegasus' has a meaning like 'the mythical winged horse'.

According to this suggestion, then, we should analyse the meaning of proper names as containing two elements: the referent (if there is one) and a description of the crucial properties the referent is taken to have. A very famous example of this kind of two-element approach to meaning comes from the German logician and philosopher Gottlob Frege. Frege was particularly concerned with *co-referential expressions*, that is to say, two or more terms which refer to a single object in the world. His favoured example involved the names 'Hesperus' and 'Phosphorus', both of which refer to one and the same celestial object, the planet Venus. A simple referential account of the meaning of these two names would hold that they *must* have the same meaning (because meaning is given by what the expression refers to and these two names both refer to the same thing). Yet this conclusion seems wrong. For someone might know both these names and yet fail to realize that they refer to the same object.

For instance, the ancient astronomers who first introduced the names took 'Hesperus' as a label for the bright star seen in the evening and 'Phosphorus' as the name for the bright star seen in the morning, without realizing that these were the same object. These speakers would have said that 'Hesperus is not Phosphorus', and they would have learnt something if they had discovered that that claim was false. This seems to entail that there must be more to the meaning of the names than their (shared) referent alone. Frege dubbed this crucial second element the name's *sense*, which is the way an object is presented when it is picked out by the name. The sense of 'Hesperus' is something like *bright star seen in the evening*, whereas the sense of 'Phosphorus' is *bright star seen in the morning*. Identity statements like 'Hesperus is Phosphorus' are thus informative because they tell us that an object thought about in one way is the same thing as an object thought about in another way. (For a contemporary example, imagine someone who is told, for the first time, that 'Peter Parker is Spiderman' (Figure 5).)

Frege's approach to the meaning of names marks an important divergence from the purely referential accounts of meaning with which this chapter began. For, whereas Mill took the meaning of a name to be exhausted by the thing in the world to which it referred,

5. Example of a single object with two names which reflect very different ways of thinking about the referent.

Frege's account takes the meaning of a name to be a complex construction, containing two different elements. (A similar point holds for the kind of indexical and demonstrative expressions we discussed earlier, since although the meaning of these words involves reference to an object—recall our example of an utterance of 'I' which refers to the speaker and not Margaret Thatcher, even if everyone in the room thinks the speaker is Margaret Thatcher— they also involve a special way of thinking about that object—recall Perry's example of the shopper with the leaky bag.)

Frege was led to the view that names must have complex meanings (made up of both a referent and a sense) because he recognized that in some contexts the way in which an object is presented or thought about matters. However, we might also be led to the same idea in other ways. For instance, the claim that word meanings are complex also emerges in linguistic theories which are concerned with explaining the formal, predictable patterns of meaning displayed by linguistic expressions.

In particular, many linguists who investigate 'lexical semantics' (i.e. the study of word meaning) posit a complex set of ideas or instructions underlying the meaning of apparently simple words. This complex structure is then used to explain and predict the different readings that sentences give rise to. Consider, for example, the following pair of sentences:

1. John is eager to please.
2. John is easy to please.

Here, despite the clear surface similarities of the sentences, it turns out each one has a very different meaning. For while (1) means that John is eager to please someone else (so John is doing the pleasing), (2) means that it is easy for someone else to please John (John is the one to be pleased). The role John plays in each case thus turns out to be diametrically opposed simply because of the meaning that attaches to 'eager' versus 'easy'.

These sorts of differences don't seem to be ones we can predict or capture simply by adopting a referential account of the meaning of the words involved: saying that the adjective 'easy' picks out a property of *easiness* doesn't seem to tell us anything about why John ends up playing different roles in (1) and (2). Yet we might expect a proper account of word meaning to explain or capture that fact.

Or again, consider so-called 'conative' constructions such as 'Jill cut at the rope'. It turns out that some expressions participate in the conative form (we can say 'Yuri kicked at the cat') while others resist it (the sentences 'Yuri touched at the cat' and 'Sam broke at the bottle' are much less acceptable in English). To capture these kinds of differences, the linguist Beth Levin has argued that we need to go beyond a referential understanding of the meaning of verbs, instead analysing their meaning as complex constructions of more basic meaning properties.

Whereas a simple referential model would suggest an account of verb meaning where we simply pair the expression with a relation in the world (yielding clauses like *'hit' refers to the property of hitting*), these theorists argue that we should treat classes of verbs as *themselves* having meaning properties. So, for instance, they suggest that we should group together verbs like 'hit', 'kick', and 'punch', as they all specify ways of making (damaging) surface contact with an object. On the other hand, verbs like 'break', 'crack', and 'shatter' all have meanings which specify types of damage that result from contact with an object. It is these underlying meaning properties which explain why 'John cracked the window' entails that the window was damaged, whereas 'John hit the window' does not.

According to this kind of lexical semantics, we can say more about the meaning of verbs like 'hit' and 'break' (and the classes they belong to) than that they simply pick out certain activities or relations in the world; and doing so will help to explain the formal meaning properties these expressions display. So, just as with Frege's account of names, the meaning of our words is held to be a complex construction containing more than simply a specification of the aspect of the world that the term picks out.

When it comes to individual words, then, we find that a pure referential approach seems just too good to be true. Sadly, it doesn't look as if we can simply find the object that pairs up neatly with each linguistic sign and leave it at that. Instead, we will have to get into the painstaking details of particular classes of expression (including adjectives like 'eager' versus adjectives like 'easy') and understand how they combine with other linguistic items (in sentences like 'John is eager to please' versus 'John is easy to please') to produce importantly different kinds of meanings. However, this doesn't spell the end for the referential account, since the meanings of full sentences might still turn out to represent the world in a relatively straightforward way.

Chapter 4
Meaning and truth

In this chapter we broaden out the referential approach to look at how the meanings of whole sentences, not just individual words, could be explained in terms of their relationship to states of the world, or to entire 'possible worlds' (or other kinds of abstract models). The theories we are interested in make a fundamental assumption about the nature of meaning in language: namely, that it can be illuminated by thinking about the conditions required to make a sentence *true*. We put our words together, the thought goes, in a way that paints a picture of reality; and meaning lies in that picturing of the world.

Spelling this metaphor out, however, requires us to think about the structure of our language, in order to discover which sentences might be made meaningful in this way and to see exactly how the envisaged picturing of reality might come about. Thus advocates of this kind of approach have suggested that we need to analyse natural language sentences in order to reveal their underlying form or structure, and then show how this structure reflects or makes claims about the world.

This kind of approach to meaning has a long history and we will start by looking at an early example of it in the work of Ludwig Wittgenstein. In the contemporary arena, an entire school of thought known as 'formal semantics' has grown up in recent decades (with influential developments coming from the logician Richard Montague, the linguist Barbara Partee, and the philosopher Donald Davidson, amongst many others). Much of the chapter will be concerned with examining this highly influential movement.

Uncovering the structure of language in the way that formal semantics requires is not straightforward, but it is a task worth undertaking, for linking meaning and truth in this way holds out the promise of capturing some key facts about meaning in language. For instance, we may be able to explain how the meaning of complex sentences (and perhaps larger texts) is a *function* of the meaning of their parts. We can also make clear why sentences have certain kinds of what we might call 'formal meaning relations', for instance why they display the kind of entailment relations that they do (e.g. what makes 'John bought a big dog' entail 'John bought a dog' but not vice versa). While at times approaches which link meaning and truth can become quite technical, it is important to remember that they have a very ambitious aim: they hope to take the complex, intricate, and creative construct that is a natural human language and render its workings entirely transparent, showing how it is the product of systematic rules which speakers (at least tacitly) grasp and apply.

Wittgenstein's picture theory of meaning

In the *Tractatus Logico-Philosophicus*, the 20th-century German philosopher Ludwig Wittgenstein argued that the function of language is to picture the world (we should note that in his later *Philosophical Investigations*, Wittgenstein adopted a very different model, one which sought to locate the meaning of linguistic expressions in their use, rather than in claims about truth). To appreciate Wittgenstein's account, it is helpful first to think about models or maps, like the map of London's underground train system (Figure 6).

6. Section of the London Underground map.

Models and maps represent states of affairs by containing some basic representational elements (say, the signs for each underground station) which hook up with core elements of the situation to be depicted (i.e. standing for the real-world stations) and they then arrange these elements in ways which mirror the relations between the elements in the real world (so that, on the London Underground map, the sign for Oxford Circus appears between the signs for Bond Street and Tottenham Court Road, just as in the real-world, Oxford Circus station falls physically between Bond St and Tottenham Court Rd stations). Models and maps thus represent by correlating basic elements with things in the world and then mirroring the relations between those objects using the structure within which the basic elements are contained.

According to Wittgenstein, meaning in language arises in exactly the same way. We can identify the basic elements of the language (roughly, words) and see that they hook up with basic objects, while the grammatical or logical structure of the language mirrors the structure of the world. This mirroring relation provides one way to understand Wittgenstein's famous remark that 'The limits of my language mean the limits of my world': every state of affairs that could exist in the world can be expressed in a meaningful statement of my language and anything that cannot be expressed in the language cannot be a possible state of the world. Sentences are true when they picture actual states of affairs (how the world really is) and they are false when they picture merely possible but unrealized states of affairs (i.e. how the world is not).

Importantly for Wittgenstein, this entails that any sentence which does not picture an actual or possible state of affairs turns out not to have any meaning at all. This led him to the radical claim that assertions about subjects like ethics or religion, or indeed philosophy itself, are, strictly speaking, nonsense—lacking all meaning or sense. His instruction, in the *Tractatus*, that 'What we cannot speak about we must pass over in silence' marks an important point of continuity between the work of the early and the later Wittgenstein, for although in his later work he adopted a very different approach to meaning, this scepticism about the claims of philosophy remained a common thread. (In his later work, he argued that the problems of philosophy are pseudo-problems, which arise when we are misled by our language and seek to use words in ways that depart from ordinary speech.)

Wittgenstein's picture theory, with its radical rejection of meaningfulness for so many claims, isn't widely adopted in the contemporary arena. Nevertheless, the core ideas his approach embodies (also closely associated with the philosophers Gottlob Frege and Bertrand Russell) have been hugely influential, eventually helping to shape a major research programme in linguistics, 'formal semantics'. According to formal semantics, just as Wittgenstein thought, we need to analyse a natural language to make clear its underlying logical structure and then we can explain meaning by seeing how this underlying structure maps to the world.

Logical form

To begin to see what formal semantics involves, note that, alongside natural languages (like English and French) there are also artificial languages, constructed by theorists, including programming languages (like Java) and logical or algebraic systems. One of the most famous of these logical languages is something called 'predicate calculus', a system developed by pioneers of mathematical logic in the late 19th and early 20th centuries, such as Charles Peirce, Bertrand Russell, and Gottlob Frege (whose theory of names we touched on in the last chapter). The purpose of a logical language is to help us identify good forms of reasoning, distinguishing good inferences, which allow us to move from one true belief to another, from bad inferences, which lead us into error.

One interesting question is whether natural languages can be translated into formal, logical languages (like predicate calculus) or not. If such a translation was possible, it would be very helpful for understanding how natural languages work and for assessing the quality of reasoning we conduct in natural languages, for the languages of logic are well understood and operate using strict, transparent rules. However, when logicians like Frege looked at natural languages, what they saw seemed far too complex (and potentially lawless) to be captured using the constrained resources of logic. Thus the idea that natural languages could be translated into formal languages seemed doomed.

To see this, consider the sentences 'Every girl is happy' and 'A cat is on the mat'. Theorists call expressions like 'every girl' and 'a cat' 'quantified phrases' because they tell us about the *quantity* of objects which have a given property (talking about *all* the girls and *one* cat respectively). The logical system Frege developed contained two logical operators designed to perform the function of quantification: one, called the 'universal quantifier', roughly captured the meaning of 'all' and 'every', and the other, labelled the 'existential quantifier', captured the meaning of 'at least one'. However, Frege's system contained just these two quantifiers, whereas natural languages have *lots* of expressions which seem to perform the same kind of function. We can say that 'every girl is happy' and that 'some girl is happy', but we can also say 'most girls are happy', 'two girls are happy', 'a few girls are happy', and so on, where all of these expressions talk about the quantity of girls who have the property of being happy. Translating all of these different expressions using the limited resources of Frege's predicate logic system turns out to be impossible (which isn't to say philosophers haven't tried: one of the most infamous bits of philosophy of language is an account of the meaning of so-called 'definite descriptions'—expressions like 'the girl' or 'the cat'—offered by British philosopher and political activist Bertrand Russell in 1905, which tries, in a very convoluted way, to capture the meaning of these kinds of terms in Frege's logical system).

One of the breakthroughs of formal semantics, then, was to show how the syntactic, or logical, structure of a sentence could be captured in a way which was much closer to the surface form of natural language sentences. In this way, theorists could lay bare the formal, structural properties of natural languages without trying to force them into the artificial straitjacket of a traditional logical language like Frege's. (It is this insight—that a natural language can be formalized without translating it into one of the limited, artificial logical languages previously available—which lies behind the title of the linguist Richard Montague's seminal paper 'English as a Formal Language'.)

In formal semantics, sentences are broken down stepwise into smaller meaningful parts. Depending on the grammatical categories of these parts (e.g. whether they are nouns, verbs, or adjectives) and the relations that hold between them (e.g. whether a noun is the subject or the object of a verb), formal semantics shows how the meaning of a whole sentence can be calculated using systematic functions of the kind used in mathematics. Once we have a statement of this form, which shows how a complex whole sentence breaks down into formally related parts, then, provided we have an account of the meaning of the basic parts of the structure (via what is known as a 'lexical entry' for each word), we can derive the meaning of the sentence.

Although the details get relatively technical quite quickly, it is easy to see the principle in practice. Take (a slightly simplified version of) the sentence introduced in Chapter 2:

Every girl petted a cat.

Using ideas developed in very influential work on syntax by the linguist Noam Chomsky, the internal relations of a sentence are often represented using a tree diagram, like the one in Figure 7

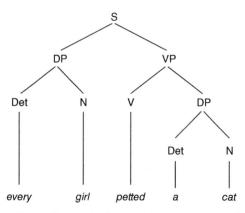

7. **A syntactic tree diagram for the English sentence 'Every girl petted a cat.'**

(where the initials stand for the following categories: 'S' = sentence, 'DP' = determiner phrase, 'VP' = verb phrase, 'Det' = determiner, 'N' = noun, NP = noun phrase).

This level of interpretation, often called a 'logical form', stands between the surface level of the sentence (i.e. its written or spoken form), on one side, and the semantic (meaning) level interpretation, on the other (we will see why logical form differs from surface form in just a moment).

While most of the syntactic categories in the above tree will be familiar to readers, 'Det' is a novel introduction within formal semantics, which (unlike prior logical systems) offers a unified account of a wide range of quantified phrases in natural language. The approach, known as 'generalized quantification', analyses expressions as comprising distinct elements: a 'determiner phrase' (such as 'every girl', 'some girls', 'many girls', 'one girl', etc.), labelled by 'DP', and a 'verb phrase' (such as 'petted a cat', 'eat avocados', or 'will win a prize'). By providing a mathematical rule for each kind of determiner, the account is able to show how we can derive the meaning of any quantified expression at all in a natural language (e.g. 'a girl is happy' requires that the number of objects in the intersection of the set of girls and the set of happy things is at least one, whereas 'most girls are happy' requires that there are more objects in the intersection of the set of girls and happy things than there are in the rest of the set of girls, and so on).

Formal semantics may seem like an excessively complex and mechanistic kind of approach, but there are huge benefits to be had from really clarifying the structural properties of sentences, for it opens the door to capturing a range of interesting facts about meaning. To see this, note that our sample sentence—'Every girl petted a cat'—is ambiguous in an interesting way (and a way that you may not have noticed on first reading). We can help to highlight the two different readings by asking 'how many cats are required for the sentence to be true?' On one interpretation, the sentence only requires *one* cat—say the very needy Kitty—with that single cat being jointly petted by every girl. On another reading, however, the sentence would only be true if every girl is petting a *different* cat: the first girl has Kitty on her lap, the second has Whiskers, and so on and so forth. (This difference in readings is known in the trade as a 'scope distinction', as it depends on which expression is taken as having the widest logical scope in the sentence—the determiner phrase on the left of our tree diagram or the one on the right.)

Different meanings like these can be captured and clarified by formal semantic analyses, which specify each reading's distinct logical properties, that is, the properties affecting its truth or falsity, and the further inferences it licenses or fails to license. So those who propose a structural analysis of scope differences (like the linguist Tanya Reinhart) claim that 'Every girl petted a cat' has two different underlying logical forms, developed from the same tree diagram: crudely, one where the phrase 'a cat' gets to go first (so that we interpret 'every girl' relative to the meaning already fixed for 'a cat', giving us the reading where the same cat is petted by every girl), and one where 'every girl' gets interpreted first and we then think about the value of 'a cat' relative to every girl (giving us the reading where each girl could have a different cat). This reveals why logical form must be treated as a *different* level of analysis to surface form, since a single surface form can have two (or more) logical forms underlying it.

Or again, consider some of the apparently weird patterns of entailment relations that we find in English (where '→' stands for 'entails' and '↛' stands for 'does not entail'):

1. John bought a dog → John bought an animal.
2. John did not buy a dog ↛ John did not buy an animal.
3. John bought a dog ↛ John bought a big dog.
4. John did not buy a dog → John did not buy a big dog.

By laying bare the logical forms of these sentences and properly understanding the role that quantifiers and expressions like 'not' play in a sentence, formal semantics is able to explain (and make entirely predictable) the patterns of entailment that we find in sentences like (1–4). We won't go any further into the details here, but one of the great attractions of the formal semantics approach is its ability to show how a range of highly complex and difficult facts about meaning in language (e.g. concerning things like tense, pronouns, relative clauses, and phrases of the form 'if... then') can be explained. The key is to understand how the syntactic elements of a sentence are arranged and what kind of rules govern the way elements within a logical form can move or relate to one another.

The formal semantics approaches we have discussed so far have focused on the sentence as the main unit of linguistic meaning—the point at which claims about the state of the world get made. However, we might think that we should cast our net even wider, focusing on larger linguistic exchanges in the form of extended discourse. This idea has been embraced by some formal semanticists who seek to model not just how the meaning of a sentence depends on the meaning of its parts and the way they are put together, but on how meaning in a conversation emerges and grows over time. These kinds of approaches, known as 'dynamic semantics' (championed by theorists like Hans Kamp and Irene Heim), seek to explain the accretion of meaning across a dialogue, showing how both the meaning of a dialogue evolves from the claims that make it up and how the meaning of the dialogue at large can influence our interpretation of parts of sentences. To take a simple example, an utterance of 'she' will be understood differently in the stand-alone sentence 'She is my daughter' and the longer dialogue 'If you go to London, make sure you meet the Mayoress. She is my daughter.' Dynamic semantics thus suggests that, in order to properly interpret pronouns and certain other expressions, we need to model the meaning of whole conversations, not merely individual sentences.

Meaning as conditions for truth

The claim so far has been that uncovering the logical form of complex linguistic expressions, and using the tools of mathematics and logic to specify the rules embodied in a natural language, can help us to capture a range of interesting meaning facts (such as why certain sentences are ambiguous, or which sentences entail which other sentences). However, we haven't yet said much about what sentence meanings *are* on a formal semantics approach. In fact, different accounts adopt rather different answers to this question, but in general formal semantics agrees with the thrust of the referential account introduced in the last chapter, holding that the place to locate meaning for a language lies in the relationship between words and what they are about (where, importantly, this is either the real world itself or some constructed model of it). Thus, within the formal semantics tradition, the idea has been that sentence meanings can be equated with what are known as 'truth conditions', that is, specifications of how the world must be if the sentence is true.

At first, the idea that truth can tell us anything about meaning may seem extraordinary. However, on reflection, there is an intuitive connection between the two notions. The linguist Max Cresswell captured this in what he called his 'Most Certain Principle': we may not know exactly what meanings are but, considering two sentences, if we can imagine a situation in which one of them is true and the other false, then we know that they do not have the same meaning.

In a similar vein, the philosopher Donald Davidson pointed out that if you were trying to teach someone a foreign language and they were able to state how the world would be if a given sentence in the new language were true, we would take that as sufficient to show that they grasped the meaning of the sentence in question. According to Davidson, then, to know the meaning of a sentence like 'John bought a dog' one has to know that this sentence is true if the person referred to by the name 'John' bought a dog, and false if he bought (only) a cat, or a hamster, or nothing at all, etc. Davidson argued, then, that we could get away without ever asking questions directly about meaning (e.g. 'what does this sentence mean?'), replacing all such questions with ones about truth (e.g. 'what would the world be like if this sentence was true?').

One worry with this kind of approach, however, is that claims about truth can sometimes come apart from claims about meaning. To see this, consider what are known as 'necessary truths': claims which are *always* true, no matter what other conditions obtain. For instance, 'Either today is Monday or it is not' is a necessary truth—however the world is, it will always be true that either today is Monday or it isn't. But now consider another necessary truth, say '2 + 2 = 4'. Once again (given certain assumptions about the nature of mathematics) it turns out that, however the world is, it is always true that $2 + 2 = 4$. Yet this means that 'Either today is Monday or it is not' and '2 + 2 = 4' both share *exactly the same* truth conditions (they turn out to be true in exactly the same set of situations, namely *all* of them). If we claim, as the truth-conditional approach to meaning does, that the meaning of a sentence is given by how the world is if that sentence is true, then all necessary truths turn out to have the *same* meaning. That conclusion is clearly not acceptable. Even if 'Either today is Monday or it isn't' and '2 + 2 = 4' are true in exactly the same situations (namely all possible situations) they certainly do not mean the same thing.

Critics of truth-conditional approaches to meaning have pointed to this, and other similar cases where there seems to be a discrepancy between meaning and truth, and argued that we can't, contra Davidson, simply replace the search for meaning with the search for truth conditions. Thus some theorists have argued that we should adopt an alternative kind of approach, one which eschews the appeal to things in the world and to conditions of truth, in favour of an appeal to thoughts or to practices. (A less radical approach, though, would be to treat truth conditions as *part of* meaning and go looking for the other ingredients we need to add.)

Locating meaning in the world versus locating meaning in the mind

Before moving on, we need to consider a final question about meaning and truth, for we need to address just how *realist* the appeal to truth conditions actually is. That is to say, is what matters for formal semantics the connection between a natural language and *the real world*, or is it rather a connection between the language and some constructed *model of the world*? This issue came up (in a slightly different way) already, in the last chapter, when we were thinking about the referents of proper names and we asked whether the only available referents were real-world objects (like people and dogs and tables), or whether the category of referents might include merely *possible* objects (like Pegasus or the non-existent person between me and the door). A similar dispute opens up now at the sentence level: do truth conditions relate to states of the real world, or to a structured model (i.e. a merely possible, theoretical construct, which might exist only in a person's head)?

This divide marks one of the most fundamental (and perhaps intractable) philosophical disputes about meaning. Advocates of a full-blooded realist approach claim that the place to locate meaning is in the relationship between linguistic signs and states of the actual world. They are thus what are called *semantic externalists*, holding that what matters for the meaning of an expression is something in the external world, something 'outside the head' of the agent, as it were. For an externalist, the meaning of the word 'dog' or the sentence 'Most dogs are loyal' is given by the fact that it refers to actual dogs in the real world, or that it picks out the real-world property of 'being a dog'. So even if someone mistakenly thinks that foxes are dogs, or that chihuahuas are not dogs, whenever they talk about dogs, they still refer to a class that includes chihuahuas and doesn't include foxes.

Semantic internalists, on the other hand, hold that the meaning of an expression is given by something within the heads of speakers: 'dog' stands for our *idea* or *concept* of dogs. So, when our confused speaker talks about dogs, they refer to a class that includes foxes but excludes chihuahuas. Although we could then go on to use this concept to categorize things in the world, when we do this we are imposing our ideas on the world rather than necessarily hooking up to objective, mind-independent features. Furthermore, for the internalist meaning comes not from this subsequent process of sorting the world into things which fall under my concept of *dog* and things which don't; rather the meaning is given by the *idea* or *concept* itself. From an internalist perspective, the specifications of meaning provided by formal semantics should be understood in terms of a constructed model ('John bought a dog' gets its meaning from expressing the thought that some individual stands in the buying relation to some dog, but where there is as yet no connection to actual objects or relations in the external world).

Semantic internalism begins to suggest that it might be a mistake to think (as the referential proposals we have looked at so far have done) that meaning in language emerges directly from the connection between language and the world. Instead, when we enquire about the meaning of people's concepts, we should really be interested in the various (true or false) beliefs they have. Take the example of someone's concept of *water*. Let's imagine that she believes water to be a clear liquid that falls as rain, fills our rivers, and quenches our thirst (amongst other things). This cluster of beliefs she holds about water is taken to constitute her concept of water and it is the connection between the word 'water' and this cluster of ideas which underpins the word's meaning.

The late 20th century saw lively debates about internalism and externalism in the philosophy of mind and language. In a 1975 essay called 'The Meaning of Meaning', the philosopher Hilary Putnam famously denied that meanings were 'in the head' and endorsed an externalist position instead. He asks us to imagine a planet, 'Twin Earth', which is exactly like Earth except that the liquid called 'water' there is not H_2O but has a different chemical composition, abbreviated to XYZ. Even though the two liquids are indistinguishable to the senses and perform identical functions in the environment, they ultimately have different essences. Putnam argues that, intuitively, on Twin Earth the word 'water' has a different meaning than on Earth—it means XYZ rather than H_2O. Moreover, this was just as true before the chemical compositions of the two liquids were known, as after: an earthling and her counterpart on Twin Earth would have believed exactly the same things about the liquid they were calling 'water' while unwittingly meaning different things by that term.

Importantly, Putnam's argument, if correct, applies equally to the contents of thoughts as to the meanings of words and sentences. Consider again the beliefs of the earthling and her Twin Earth counterpart. What are these beliefs really about? According to the externalist, whenever the earthling believes, say, that *water is wet*, she is having a belief about something with the chemical composition H_2O. In contrast, whenever the twin earther believes that *water is wet*, she is having a belief about something with the chemical composition XYZ. Thus, the very contents of their thoughts vary with their environments.

The upshot of Putnam's externalism is the following: wherever thoughts are about physical entities in the world, the precise constitution of those entities determines the precise constitution of the corresponding thoughts. So, even though both twin earthers believe the same things about the liquid they call 'water', their respective water-concepts differ in meaning. The philosopher Tyler Burge later took the idea one step further. Moving from the physical world to the social realm, he argued that the contents of our thoughts can also depend on how experts in a linguistic community define relevant terms.

We can see how externalism about mental contents echoes the referential accounts of linguistic meaning we have been considering. Like those accounts, content externalism identifies bits of the (physical or social) world as meanings. This time, though, they are taken to constitute meanings in the mind, as well as meanings in language. In effect, then, content externalism builds the world in one step earlier than the referential models we have looked at so far, at the level of thought. Semantic internalism, on the other hand, holds that we do not need to look beyond the mind of an individual to specify meaning: meanings are, contra Putnam, 'all in the head'.

The debate between externalism and internalism is entrenched and it is hard to see what would constitute a knock-down argument in either direction, but both approaches highlight a potential shift in our thinking about meaning: rather than focusing directly on meaning in language, perhaps we should instead consider meaning in thought. In the next two chapters, we explore what this move might entail for our understanding of meaning.

Chapter 5
Meaning and concepts

According to some theorists, meaning is not just a matter of hanging labels on bits of the world (the approach of Chapter 3) or modelling states of affairs (the approach of Chapter 4). Instead, we need a theory which can capture a kind of meaning words can have where this *differs* from what they pick out in the world. So, for instance, we need an account of meaning which explains how someone can rationally believe that Marilyn Monroe starred in the film *Some Like it Hot*, while disbelieving that Norma Jeane Mortenson starred in *Some Like it Hot*, even though Marilyn was in fact the same person as Norma Jeane (with 'Marilyn Monroe' being her stage name). To cope with this kind of case it seems we need to consider the *ideas* that speakers associate with the name 'Marilyn Monroe' versus the *ideas* that they associate with 'Norma Jeane'. Rather than looking to the world for meaning (or at least, in addition to looking to the world), we need to look to the minds of language users to provide linguistic meaning.

Complex word meanings

In fact, we have already looked at an account which begins to lead us in this direction. For in Chapter 3 we looked at the philosopher Gottlob Frege's idea that the meaning of a name was composed of two different elements (which Frege termed *sense* and *reference*, or more accurately, since questions have been raised about how to

translate Frege's original German terms, *Sinn* and *Bedeutung*).
Frege held that the meaning of a name like 'Salzburg' would not be
completely exhausted by the city it names but could include other
things we know or believe about the city—say, that it is the
birthplace of Mozart. Thus, in addition to the referent, Frege held
names convey a *sense*, an aspect of content which tells us how the
user of the name is thinking about the referent. Frege's distinction
between sense and reference allowed him to solve various puzzles
that names give rise to, like the problem of empty names or how the
claim that 'Hesperus is Phosphorus' can be informative even though
the two names share a single referent. It remains a little murky,
though, exactly how we should think of the notion of sense.

Frege himself thought of senses as being *objective* rather than
subjective phenomena, meaning that they are not just a
proliferation of idiosyncratic ideas in the heads of individual
language users but are instead shared across a linguistic
community. Frege also thought of senses as being *abstract* rather
than *concrete*, meaning that they could not be identified with
tangible real-world entities, like objects, people, or places.
Unfortunately, these twin characteristics—objectivity and
abstractness—have made it quite difficult to understand exactly
what Frege's senses could actually be.

Subsequent philosophers have tried to demystify the notion of
sense in one way or another, taking Frege's basic insight but
developing it in different ways. Most often, they have reinterpreted
senses as *psychological* entities, relaxing Frege's strict objectivity
constraint (and also his abstractness constraint, to the extent that
psychological entities are considered to be non-abstract things,
perhaps being thought of as neural or other physical states).
On this view, the sense of a word or sentence consists in the
thoughts or ideas that speakers have in using it. After all, it is quite
natural to think that the difference between the meanings of
'Hesperus' and 'Phosphorus' for the early astronomers boils down
to what they *believed* these words referred to. In particular, they

were assuming the existence of two objects with two distinct sets of properties: one was visible in the morning, the other in the evening. This points to the meaning of a word being constituted (at least in part) by what it brings to mind—the underlying idea, or concept, it evokes. On this approach, meaning is at least partly a matter of what goes on in the minds of language users, not just what (if anything) a word corresponds to in the world.

A common way of thinking about senses, then, is as descriptions that individuals believe to be true of an object they have in mind. So, the sense of 'Hesperus' for the early astronomers would have included a description like 'The star that is visible in the evening, not the morning' (and vice versa for 'Phosphorus'). Since the early astronomers believed different things about the referents of 'Hesperus' and 'Phosphorus' (e.g. concerning the time of day at which each was visible) the two names ended up having different senses.

A descriptive approach is not the only option. For instance, another recent psychological account, put forward by the philosopher François Recanati, builds sense into the architecture, rather than the contents, of our thoughts. Recanati thinks of senses as 'mental files' in which we store information about objects in our environment. This would be to understand the early astronomers as storing information about Hesperus/Phosphorus in two separate mental files. When it was eventually discovered that all the information they had gathered concerned only a single object, astronomers had to merge their mental files into one, thereby coming to represent the world more accurately. Whichever kind of psychological approach is ultimately preferred, the key point is that there is something about the subjective states of speakers that imbues their words with meanings, in excess of what they pick out in the world.

While we might take the meaning of an expression to be a complex construction, including both appeal to things in the world and appeal to things in the mind, a bolder proposal would be to treat the psychological component as giving the *complete* meaning of the expression. In this way, the meaning of an expression would be given, not by the thing in the world to which it refers, but entirely by the kinds of ideas and thoughts it generates.

Conceptual role semantics

One concrete attempt to spell meaning out in this way comes from a position known as 'conceptual role' semantics. According to conceptual role semantics, to know the meaning of an expression is to know how it relates to other ideas. To see this, think about what you need to know to be a competent user of the English word 'dog'. It seems that, if you have grasped the meaning of this term, then the sentence 'Fido is a dog' will be linked in your mind with claims like *Fido is an animal, Fido probably has four legs, Fido probably barks and is furry*, etc. Perhaps, then, we could just take the meaning of 'dog' to be composed of these kinds of conceptual links—the cluster of ideas that someone associates with the word. On this model the meaning of a word *just is* the complete, complex conceptual network within which the expression sits (see Figure 8).

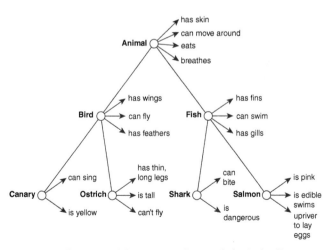

8. An example of part of the conceptual network for 'animal'.

(This kind of approach can also be couched at the level of language use, rather than directly at the level of thought. We will touch on that version, known as 'inferential role semantics', when we look at the claim that meaning is use in Chapter 7.)

An immediate threat to this kind of approach, however, is the risk that it will end up relativizing meaning in language to individuals. For instance, let's say that I have a pet dog called 'Bonzo'. When I hear the sentence 'Fido is a dog' I'm disposed to think that *Fido and Bonzo are the same kind of animal*. However, assuming that you don't know anything about Bonzo's existence, that's not an idea you are going to be disposed to entertain. If we decide to treat meaning as fixed by the complete, complex bundle of ideas that an individual associates with an expression, we will end up concluding that 'dog' means something different in my mouth from what it means in yours (since the bundle of ideas I associate with 'dog' differs from the bundle that you associate with the word). While some theorists have been willing to accept this (holding that all that is required for linguistic communication to succeed is some kind of *similarity* of meaning), others have seen it as a real problem.

Would it be possible to adopt a conceptual role model of meaning but avoid the idea that signs simply mean different things for different people (whenever they associate different ideas with the same sign, based on their unique background experiences and personalities)? The obvious way to do this would be to claim that *not all associated ideas carry the same weight*. Instead, we might suppose that meaning is fixed by a core subset of the inferences someone is willing to draw, while inferences outside this core are treated as just idiosyncratic, non-meaning-constituting connections. For instance, we might think that the meaning of 'dog' is constituted (in part) by the fact that speakers who hear 'Fido is a dog' will be disposed to think that *Fido is an animal* and *Fido probably barks*, while the move from 'Fido is a dog' to *Fido and Bonzo are the same kind of animal* turns out just to be a personal, idiosyncratic association of ideas, which cannot influence the meaning of the public sign 'dog'.

Clearly, however, the crucial task for this kind of approach is to specify *which* are the important (i.e. meaning-constituting) inferences and which are the unimportant ones. This leads us into a historically very significant (but also extremely vexed) debate in philosophy, concerning the possibility of what is known as 'conceptual analysis' (which aims to analyse the contents of our concepts, a task some have taken to be the primary goal of philosophy) and the distinction between what are known as 'analytic' versus 'synthetic' claims.

'Analytic claims' are those which are held to be true in virtue of their meaning alone, while 'synthetic claims' are made true by the meaning of expressions *plus* how the world is. So, for instance, 'All bachelors are unmarried' is held to be made true just by the meanings of 'bachelor' and 'unmarried', hence it is an analytic claim (as are 'All vixens are female foxes' and 'A puppy is a young dog'). On the other hand, 'All bachelors are rich' is true or false depending on how the world is and so is synthetic. (Analytic truths have held a special place in philosophy as they have been thought to provide a special source of knowledge—a priori knowledge—which could be had independently from any investigation of how things are in the external world. So, for instance, mathematical truths have often been thought to be knowable a priori.)

In order for the kind of conceptual role semantics we are considering here to get off the ground, it seems we need a firm divide between analytic claims (which provide core, meaning-constituting inferences) and synthetic claims (the inferences which will depend on people's background experience and information, and so do not serve as meaning-constituting). However, whether the analytic/synthetic divide can really be drawn, and thus whether relations between ideas can really give us the meaning of words in a public language, continues to be much debated amongst philosophers. Accordingly, the jury is out on the prospects for conceptual role semantics.

Polysemy

Another area of focus for mentalistic approaches to meaning has been *polysemous* words, that is, words which possess a network of related meanings. For example, we can talk about a 'book' as a physical object with a particular size and weight, which can be placed on a shelf or packed in a bag. But we can also think of a 'book' in terms of its content, which could equally well be downloaded to an e-reader or awarded a literary prize. Note that what is happening here is different from mere ambiguity, where a single written, spoken, or signed form has multiple meanings (like 'jumper' meaning an item of clothing or one who jumps). In cases of polysemy it is no accident that the word has the different meanings it has, as is evident from the fact that it has them in other languages too.

One way to understand polysemy is to treat word meanings as complex bundles of ideas, with certain elements of that bundle being stressed or de-emphasized in a given use of the term. So, in some uses of 'book' we foreground ideas like 'is a concrete object' and 'has a certain physical location', while in the other we foreground ideas like 'is an abstract object' and 'is a story' (this approach has been developed in detail by the computer scientist James Pustejovsky and the linguist Ray Jackendoff). Like the general 'conceptual role semantics' we looked at earlier, this approach takes the meaning of a word to be given by a complex, hierarchical conceptual structure, though for the different senses of a polysemous term we might be somewhat less concerned about the problem of relativizing meanings to individuals (which we saw beset the conceptual role model as a general account of word meaning).

One reason we might be less concerned is that polysemous senses apparently come in a range, from the most predictable, regular ones (like the two senses of 'lamb' or 'chicken', meaning creature or meat, or the use of 'leg' for a human leg and a table leg) through to highly idiosyncratic, context-dependent ones (such as metaphorical senses of polysemous words, as in 'he was an open book' or Jesse Lee Bennett's claim that 'Books are the compasses and telescopes and sextants and charts which other men have prepared to help us navigate the dangerous seas of human life'). Given this range, regular polysemy might be taken to depend on a common or widely shared association of ideas, while the more ad hoc, context-sensitive interpretations depend on the particular context in which the term is used, and the particular associations between ideas that the speaker and hearer are willing to draw.

What all the above accounts share is a focus on the structure and contents of speakers' minds as the source of meaning for the linguistic expressions they use. More broadly, the second half of the 20th century saw a pronounced 'psychological turn' in the study of language, where it was held that we should look to the mind to answer questions about meaning in language.

Meaning in language as meaning in thought

One famous proponent of the psychological turn was the American philosopher and cognitive scientist Jerry Fodor. Fodor claimed that meaning in language was dependent on a more fundamental kind of meaning: meaning in thought. But to explain the expressive properties of natural languages (the range and scope of meanings we can express in languages like English, Farsi, or Swahili), he held that the thoughts underpinning linguistic expressions must *themselves* be language-like in crucial ways. His idea is known as the 'Language of Thought' hypothesis: the claim that thinking has the structure of linguistic representation (or, more catchily, that thoughts are sentences in the head).

The Language of Thought (sometimes labelled 'Mentalese') is not supposed to be a natural language (like French or Malay) but it is held to share two key features with natural languages: first, it contains basic building blocks. Just as words are the basic building blocks of a natural language, so concepts are the basic building blocks of Mentalese. What makes words in natural language meaningful on this model is that they hook up with concepts of Mentalese (and we'll see in a moment what makes those concepts meaningful); so the word 'dog' is held to be meaningful because it expresses the concept DOG (we'll follow a standard practice in philosophy and capitalize a word when it is standing for a concept).

Second, Fodor held that just as the meaning of a whole sentence depends on the meaning of the words it contains and the way they are put together, so the meaning of a whole thought is a function of the concepts that make it up and the way in which they are put together. The process of combining concepts together to make whole thoughts is held to be rule-governed and predictable; someone who can think HOMER LOVES MARGE can also think MARGE LOVES HOMER, since the latter thought is simply a rearrangement of the parts of the former thought. Thus thoughts are *compositional*. It is this compositionality of thought which explains, according to Fodor, our amazing ability to express and to understand an indefinite number of novel natural language sentences.

Clearly, though, if words are meaningful because they attach to concepts, it would be nice to know what makes concepts meaningful, or what makes one concept have the particular content that it does. We started out with the question of what it is for our words and sentences to have meaning, but the idea that meanings ultimately flow from the minds of thinking beings pushes this problem upstream. Now we have to ask: what is it for our *thoughts* to have meanings? Trying to answer that question has led philosophers of mind and language to undertake more detailed investigations into the nature of mental contents—what our thoughts are about and what it is for thoughts to be about things (to have 'aboutness' or 'intentionality').

One possible answer to the question of meaning at the level of thought would be to bring the world back in at this juncture and appeal to the causal relations between things in the world, on one side, and thoughts on the other. This is the approach Fodor favoured. According to Fodor, my concept DOG is about dogs because it stands in the right causal relation to dogs; for example the presence of dogs in my environment triggers the concept DOG in my mind, while the presence of horses in my environment triggers my concept HORSE, etc. This brings us back to the referential approach to meaning, for although words now get their meaning from elements at the level of thought (i.e. concepts), Fodor maintains that concepts get their content from their relations to things in the world. We appear to have come full circle: having allowed that meanings might depend on what we think, not just on what we refer to, Fodor tells us that what we think depends on what we refer to anyway!

As it stands, however, this simple causal picture is not sufficient to explain why a given concept has the content that it does. To see this, think about the conditions under which you have DOG thoughts. It is right that *sometimes* your DOG thoughts are caused by the presence of dogs, but sometimes they are caused by other things, like people talking about dogs, or by a sheep that you mistake for a dog in the fog, or by even more random features of your environment (maybe the coat someone is wearing reminds you of the shaggy hound you had as a child). Yet if, as the causal approach recommends, we spell out the content of a concept in terms of the things that cause someone to entertain that concept, we will end up having to say that the concept DOG stretches to include sheep and jackets (and who knows what else besides).

This point perhaps becomes clearer when we ask what is involved in *mis*applying a concept: we would like to say that someone who thinks to themselves 'that is a DOG' when they see a sheep in the fog is going wrong or making a mistake (they are misapplying the concept DOG). But if the simple causal approach were right, and if this person is unlucky enough to have encountered a blurry sheep before and thought to themselves DOG on that occasion, then, when they apply DOG to the blurry sheep on this occasion it turns out they are *not* making a mistake. For their concept DOG has been caused in the past by *both* dogs *and* blurry sheep (so that the content of the concept DOG is, for them, really 'dog or blurry sheep').

The attempt to defend a broadly causal account of the meaning of concepts in light of this kind of worry pushed Fodor to ever more complicated and (many have suggested) implausible accounts of how concepts get their meaning (leading the psychologist Steven Pinker to comment, in a remark he credits to philosopher Dan Dennett, 'Fodor is like a trampoline: you jump on him and he springs back, presenting claims twice as trenchant and outrageous. If some of us can see further, it's from jumping on Jerry').

This is another point at which the fundamental debate, noted at the end of Chapter 4, between externalism and internalism crops up. Those who think meaning must lie, in some way, in the relations between thoughts and the world are likely to maintain that there must be some way to spell out the necessary relationship between concepts and worldly things. Meanwhile, those who feel more sanguine about the internalist possibility that meaning lies entirely within the head of a person, so to speak, are likely to hold that we should (at least as far as questions of meaning are concerned) let go of the world and focus entirely on the thinker.

Having looked for meaning in the world and in individuals' minds, we have found ourselves caught in a dilemma: the meanings of our words and sentences can't always be given by things out there in the world, but attempting to isolate meaning as occurring solely in our thoughts makes it hard to put mind and world back in contact with one another. This dilemma constitutes perhaps *the* central problem when we try to think about meaning and it is one we will need readers themselves to reflect on, rather than hoping to settle the dispute here. Finally, however, there is an alternative connection between psychology (concepts and thoughts), on the one hand, and natural language (words and sentences), on the other, which we should be aware of.

Meaning in thought as meaning in language

The proposal in the earlier parts of this chapter was to ground the meaning of linguistic items in thought, so that words and sentences get their meanings from the concepts and thoughts they are used to express. However, not all theorists believe that the dependence goes this way round. Alternatively, some have suggested that meaning in thought depends on meaning in language—what we can *think* depends on what we can *say*. This kind of view is most famously associated with the early 20th-century American linguist Benjamin Lee Whorf (and his mentor, Edward Sapir), who wrote about so-called 'linguistic relativity' or 'linguistic determinism'.

To give a rather hackneyed (and contested) example, linguistic determinism holds that because the Inuit have so many more words for snow than English speakers do, Inuits are able to think more kinds of thoughts about snow than English speakers can. Or again, since the languages of some nomadic tribes apparently lack a complex number vocabulary (e.g. some languages seem to have words only for one, two, and many) speakers of these languages are unable to think complex thoughts involving number (according to linguistic determinism, their language prevents them from *thinking* 'there are four dogs', not just from *saying* it).

Recently, many interesting studies of linguistic relativity have been conducted by the cognitive scientist Lera Boroditsky. She finds evidence, for example, that the different ways in which speakers of

English and Mandarin talk about time (as extending horizontally or vertically) affects how they conceptualize the past, present, and future, and that a person's colour vocabulary affects the speed with which they can categorize (and recall) different shades of colour. In the philosophical arena, the idea that meaning in thought is somehow dependent on meaning in language has been endorsed by some famous thinkers. For instance, the British philosopher Michael Dummett and the American Donald Davidson both held the sweeping view that thought without language is impossible. Others have defended a more constrained approach, perhaps holding that natural language is required for *certain kinds* of thought or that language is necessary to enable people to *identify* or *attribute* thoughts to others. For instance, the philosopher and cognitive scientist Peter Carruthers has argued that conscious thought takes the form of 'inner speech' and that this takes place in a natural language (so that French speakers consciously reason in French, while Mandarin speakers consciously think in Mandarin, etc.).

Seeking to ground the meaning of our thoughts in the meaning of public words and sentences, however, clearly only advances the understanding of meaning per se if we *also* have an account of what it is for a word or sentence of a natural language to be meaningful. So, even if one is taken by the perspective of linguistic determinism (or the similar approaches touched on in this section), the hunt for an account of meaning in language must go on. Thus, in the next chapter, we explore the idea that meaning in language might be explained in terms of what a speaker intends or aims to communicate.

Chapter 6
Meaning and intentions

The last chapter focused on the idea that we could specify the meaning of words by appealing to the concepts they link up with (either individual mental representations or conceptual networks). In this chapter we turn to a somewhat different appeal to the mental realm, where meaning is held to lie in the thoughts speakers intend to convey. According to this approach, any human sign (paradigmatically, linguistic signs, but also pictures, maps, signals—anything we take to be meaningful) gets its meaning from the *communicative intention* that lies behind its production. The ringing bell means that class is about to start, the picture of the person with a walking stick means that elderly people may be crossing here, the utterance 'The cat is on the mat' means that the cat is on the mat, and in each case this is because that is the content these signs are intended—by people—to express.

One theorist who appealed to the mental realm in this way was the philosopher Paul Grice, who developed a very well-known form of what has come to be called 'intention-based semantics'. For Grice, the meaning of an utterance is given by the thought that the speaker who utters it wants to convey to their hearers. What matters for Grice's account are the meanings we intend to communicate to others, through our use of linguistic and other signs.

Intentions and speaker meaning

One of the most influential aspects of Grice's philosophy of language was his recognition that the meaning speakers convey often differs from the standing meaning of the sentences they produce (we saw an example of this right at the start of the book, with the case of Derek Bentley's alleged utterance of 'Let him have it') and his work made a major contribution to our understanding of how this happens. He identified a wholly new category of communicated meanings, which he dubbed 'implicatures'. What is distinctive of implicatures is that they cannot be decoded simply on the basis of word meanings and combinatory rules. Instead, we have to take into account all sorts of other things we know about people and the world.

Consider someone who, replying to a dinner invitation, says, 'I have to work.' The speaker is not using an idiom, nor are they being ironic, sarcastic, metaphorical, or hyperbolic (where these all seem fairly conventional ways of getting across a divergent speaker meaning). Nevertheless, this is still an instance of communicating beyond conventional meaning. The speaker does not give a straight yes or no, yet it is clear that the invitation has been declined. We know this because we can join the dots: the utterance can only be taken as a relevant and informative response if the speaker has to work *at the time when the dinner is taking place*. So, it is impossible for the speaker to attend the dinner and the response to the invitation is (a polite) 'no'.

Similarly, imagine that a musical performance is described as follows: 'The singer produced a series of sounds corresponding closely to the score.' Here, the speaker's words point towards some extra information that is not made explicit, namely that the singer gave a *bad* performance. It is the precise choice of words (and their unnecessary prolixity) that leads to this message being conveyed. If the singer had been better, the speaker surely would have used a less convoluted formulation.

Grice was interested in how occasion-specific speaker meaning outstrips the constant, conventional meanings of language, arguing that successful communication depends ultimately on our ability to make rational inferences about a speaker's purposes in uttering the words they do in the context they are in. He claimed that, as long as we assume speakers are being *cooperative* conversational partners, it is possible to figure out what they mean to communicate. That is to say, for communication to work, we need to assume that speakers are trying to convey things that are (at least believed by those speakers to be) true, informative, relevant, and clearly expressed.

Thinking again about the example above, the utterance of 'I have to work' would be a total non sequitur if we did not think about it as answering the question 'Do you want to have dinner?' Assuming the speaker's response to the dinner invitation is intended to be informative and relevant is what allows us to infer what was not said directly, namely that the invitation is being declined. Meanwhile, assuming that speakers normally opt for clear, straightforward language allows us to infer something extra from the convoluted description of the singer's performance. By relying on the 'principles of good communication' which Grice articulated (such as 'Be relevant', 'Give the amount of information your hearer needs, not more or less', 'Be truthful') we are able to work out the messages speakers intend to convey even where these diverge significantly from the standing meaning of the sentences they utter.

There have been various challenges to the idea that speakers really need to be cooperative (or that audiences need to assume they are) in order for implicatures to be worked out. Still, the core of the Gricean view remains: what we do when presented with a linguistic utterance is to try to discern the speaker meaning that lies behind it—the content that the speaker had it in mind to convey. This central idea has been developed in fruitful ways in the contemporary arena, by linguists like Larry Horn, Stephen Levinson, Ruth Kempson, Deirdre Wilson, and Robyn Carston.

One development of the broadly intentionalist project that has gained growing prominence over the last few decades is 'Relevance Theory', originally put forward by Dan Sperber and Deirdre Wilson. It analyses communication in terms of *cognitive efficiency*. The basic idea is that our brains are set up to maximize the acquisition of useful information while minimizing the associated processing costs. This principle underpins language production and comprehension, explaining why speakers make particular utterances and why audiences form particular interpretations of those utterances.

Both the Gricean project and Relevance Theory recognize that the conventional meanings of words and sentences form just one part of meaning in language. Exactly what kind of part that is remains a hotly debated question in the philosophy of language but to get an initial sense of the debate consider the following sentences:

Meaning

- I'm ready.
- Moeen has had enough.
- The apple is red.

Each of these is acceptable as a sentence of English, but working out exactly what meaning we should assign to them turns out to be difficult. The speaker who utters the first sentence won't normally communicate simply that *they are ready*, instead they are likely to convey a richer content, for example that *they are ready for the exam* or *ready for dinner*, etc. The same goes for 'Moeen has had enough', where we need to find out from the context of utterance exactly what the speaker thinks Moeen has had enough of.

Although the final sentence appears at first blush to be more complete than the other two, notice that it too can yield different interpretations when uttered; for instance, is the speaker saying that the apple is red on its skin or that it has red flesh? As with our earlier examples, utterances of these sentences can apparently convey more than the content recovered from word meaning and structure alone, but beyond this point of agreement, theorists differ about how to think about these richer meanings.

A key question is: what is the speaker committed to by uttering these sentences? For instance, imagine a context where we are waiting for Maya in order to go out for dinner and she calls out from the living room, 'I'm ready.' We might assume that Maya is saying that she is ready to leave, but in fact Maya has got confused about the plans and thinks we are bringing dinner for her, so she intends to let us know that she is ready for the food to be brought in. On one approach, if we think that the meaning of linguistic items is always, or very often, sensitive to the context in which those expressions are uttered (a position often labelled 'contextualism') we will hold that what Maya says is either that *she's ready to leave* or that *she's ready for the food to come in* (depending on whether we take the content in the mind of speakers or hearers as ultimately responsible for settling questions of meaning). Whichever claim it is she asserts, however, this meaning goes beyond the simple, context-free, compositional content *I'm ready*.

On the other hand, if we believe that we should maintain a clear difference between the standing meaning of a sentence and the things that can be conveyed by uttering it (a position known as 'semantic minimalism', defended by Emma Borg, amongst others), we might hold that Maya literally expresses only the very minimal content that *she is ready for something or other*, with the contextually enriched content (that she is ready to leave, or ready for dinner, etc.) just being what she, as a speaker, means (on a par with the speaker who declines the dinner invitation).

It might seem as if this debate is not terribly important (what does it matter, we might wonder, if a content is conveyed literally and directly or only as an indirect implicature?). However, as we saw in Chapter 2, any decision we make here has potentially significant practical repercussions. For instance, imagine that we need to determine whether Maya was lying or telling the truth when she said what she did. In order to do that, we will need to know which of these possible contents she asserted. Or again, recall the case of *Smith v. United States* (1993), where Smith was found guilty of having used a gun in pursuit of a crime when they traded the gun for drugs (rather than firing the weapon). The prosecution in this case relied on a very minimal understanding of the meaning of 'use', rejecting a more contextually salient interpretation such as *used in the stereotypical sense relating to firearms*. So, deciding whether meaning should be understood in a minimal or more contextual way really matters.

Intentions and standing meaning

Although what the speaker intends to convey is important, there is a potential danger in shifting our focus too narrowly towards speaker meaning, for we risk losing sight of one of the main tasks for a theory of meaning to perform. In Chapter 1, we saw that a puzzle about meaning concerned how to account for our (prima facie surprising) ability to understand and to produce an apparently indefinite number of novel sentences. We termed this the *productivity puzzle* and suggested that it could be solved by appeal to the compositionality of language, that is, by the fact that language has discrete building blocks that can be used and reused in rule-governed ways. But this solution depends on the building blocks staying the same across different compositions of them. Otherwise, we would have to learn the meaning of each possible use one by one and the productivity puzzle becomes intractable again. That is to say, we can explain the fact that someone who understands 'Homer loves Marge' is likely to understand 'Marge loves Homer' if we think that the meaning of the second sentence is made up of the very same elements as the first sentence, simply arranged in a different way. However we will lose that explanation if the meaning of 'Homer', 'Marge', and 'loves' is something which can vary every time they are used.

Now, the more importance we give speaker meaning over the standing meanings of words and sentences, the more variable the meanings that words and sentences end up taking on. As we have seen, what a speaker means by a word can differ wildly from its conventional meaning. So how do audiences manage to understand novel meanings if the components of meaning are so fluid and changeable? Is it really feasible that we store in our heads rules governing the entire plethora of different things speakers can say and do with their words in all actual and possible contexts? If not, how is it that we manage to communicate successfully?

This tension between the need for a stable, rule-based system, on one hand (to account for how we learn a language, and understand and make novel utterances), versus the need for a creative, flexible, and changeable system on the other (to accommodate shifts and changes in meaning, and our abilities with metaphor and other figures of speech), marks one of the most fundamental difficulties in providing an adequate account of meaning in language.

Grice's overall aim was to explain standing meaning in terms of speaker meaning (reducing meaning in language to meaning in thought), with the hope that ultimately speakers' intentions might themselves turn out to be reducible to claims about purely physical (e.g. brain) states. In this way, Grice offered a unified approach to meaning. Moreover, he hoped that it would be possible to find a place for meaning within the ordinary, physical scheme of things (so that meaning might ultimately be captured by our scientific theories of the natural world). He focused his own efforts on the first stage of this reduction, trying to show how we could reduce meaning in language to meaning in thought.

A first step in this reductive project is to claim that the meaning of any utterance is given by the thought the speaker intends the audience to form. For instance, an utterance of the sentence 'Every tall girl petted a cat' means that *every tall girl petted a cat* because what the speaker intends to convey is the thought that (the speaker believes that) every tall girl petted a cat. There are two main problems with this seemingly uncontroversial proposal: first, the relationship between intending to convey a thought and what a sign means is much more complex than this simple proposal allows; second, focusing on individual speakers risks overlooking the important role of community-wide linguistic conventions.

First, imagine that I witness a house being burgled and I want people to know about it. My intention is to have you form the belief that the house has been broken into and in order to bring this about I take a photograph of the burglar climbing in through the window and leave it lying around (see Figure 9). When you later come across the photo you do indeed come to believe that the house has been broken into. Yet intuitively, I didn't mean that the house has been broken into by leaving the photo where you could find it. What we have here is a case where I intend you to believe something—and you go on to form that very belief—but the reason you do so is merely because of the evidence I have left

9. Image of a burglar climbing through a window.

lying around for you to see, not because I produced a meaningful sign which you understood.

In contrast, if I said to you, 'You've been burgled,' you would need to understand what I meant (and believe me) in order to arrive at the conclusion that you have been burgled. The difference between these two cases is that, when I say something, I intend you to form a belief *on the basis of recognizing that very intention.* You have to treat me as someone trying to convey information to you, and not just as a producer of random noises. In the photograph case, on the contrary, my intentions were irrelevant—you formed the belief that the house had been broken into without any recognition of my intentions.

What this case seems to show is that if we want to reduce meaning in language to speaker intentions, we need to specify a tighter connection between what the speaker intends to convey, the utterance the speaker produces, and the belief the audience forms. The audience needs to endorse (or at least entertain) the belief the speaker intended them to because they *recognize the speaker's intention to convey that belief.* For genuinely meaningful action, then, it looks as if we need a notion of *intention recognition*: the reason the audience forms a belief must be because they recognize that this was the message the speaker wanted to convey.

Unfortunately, while this move gets round some of the problems, the challenges for the intention-based view don't stop there. It turns out that for each putative analysis of intention recognition, it is possible to construct a counter-example (i.e. a situation where the psychological criteria are met but the claims about linguistic meaning are not). Historically, this launched intention-based views into ever more complex epicycles of psychological proposals (trying to tie the belief formed by the hearer and the intention had by the speaker ever more tightly) which were in turn met by putative counter-examples, leading to even more complex proposals. We won't go into all the details here. The upshot is that opponents of the Gricean project to reduce meaning in language to speaker intentions have concluded that meaning is unlikely to be reducible to psychological states. At the very least, it is clear that the appealing simplicity of the intention-based account pretty quickly dissipates. The ensuing complexity has also led opponents to question whether the approach ends up being simply too complicated to explain how meaning in language comes about (particularly when we start thinking about language acquisition and how children might come to understand the meaning of what is said to them).

The second difficulty for the reduction of standing meaning to speaker intentions is one about *which* speaker intentions matter, and to what. For there are different ways in which an appeal to the thoughts and intentions of sign users might go. On the one hand, we could look at the thoughts which a specific speaker has, on a specific occasion, which leads them to produce a given sign. On the other hand, however, we could look at the kinds of intentions people *standardly* have when they produce a sign of a given type (corresponding to its standing, or conventional, meaning). This distinction matters because the two can come apart.

Suppose that when I uttered 'The cat is on the mat' yesterday, the particular thought which led me to make that utterance was that *my cat, Kitty, is on the mat in the hall*. I was also prompted to make the utterance by a hope that my partner would know that Kitty sits there when she wants to be let out and that he would, therefore, open the door for her. Obviously, however, we don't want to treat all of those very specific thoughts as contributing to the standing meaning of the English sentence 'The cat is on the mat', for others can certainly use this expression without saying anything about Kitty and without issuing the kind of indirect door-opening request that underpinned my utterance.

Or again, take the utterance attributed to Revd Spooner (from whom we get the term 'Spoonerism'): 'you have tasted two worms'.

Spooner apparently intended to express the belief that the undergraduate he was addressing had wasted two terms, but he was prone to misspeaking and confusing his words. As a result, Spooner's communicative intentions often came apart from the meanings of the sentences he actually ended up articulating.

We can even imagine that the student in fact misheard Spooner and, thinking that he uttered 'you have wasted two terms', formed the (correct) belief that Spooner thinks they have wasted two terms. Here we have a case where the speaker intended his audience to form a belief, his addressee has formed the belief in question, and has formed it on the basis of what the speaker meant, but nevertheless we don't want to assign the sentence 'you have tasted two worms' the standing meaning *you have wasted two terms*. Indeed, we don't want standing meanings to be influenced in any way by such idiosyncrasies as Spoonerisms.

The worry here mirrors one that we saw beset the conceptual role model of meaning in the last chapter. By focusing on what the speaker intends to convey, we are at risk of relativizing meaning to particular speakers, without due regard for the public, shared, and context-insensitive features of linguistic meaning. This is not to say that the particular intentions speakers have when they produce an utterance are of no help whatsoever, for, as we will see, such an appeal can definitely help when we are thinking about the very particular contents that speakers are able to communicate. However, if we are thinking about the meaning of words and other signs *in general*, it seems we need to focus not on the particular, potentially pretty ad hoc thoughts that can lead to their production. Rather we need to focus on the kinds of intentions people *standardly* have when they produce utterances of a given type.

When people say, 'The cat is on the mat,' they standardly mean to produce the belief in their speakers that *there is a cat on the mat*, a more general belief than that *Kitty is on the mat*, or *Tiddles is on the mat*, etc. Or again, although not much used, we might expect that the intentions conventionally associated with the sentence 'You have tasted two worms' alludes to worms and not terms. To give the standing meaning of an expression, the suggestion thus is, we need to look to the *conventional intentions* that go along with its production—the intentions speakers commonly have when they use it.

Again, however, this move is not without its problems. We've actually just touched on one worry, for (given the incredible capacity speakers have for expressing novel thoughts in language) we might wonder, for some sentences (like 'You have tasted two worms'), whether there really is such a thing as the *conventional intention* associated with them. Another potential problem concerns the very idea of a *linguistic convention*, since it is hard to state what these conventions are or what's required for them. For instance, how many speakers have to conform to a particular way of using an expression (and how often) in order for it to count as conventional? While many philosophers have been attracted by the idea that languages are rooted in conventions (most notably David Lewis, who uses the technical machinery of game theory to model the development of linguistic conventions) it is not straightforward to define and delineate these.

Speech acts

Similar issues crop up when we think about what speakers (deliberately or inadvertently) *do* with their words, beyond what they intend to communicate with them. One way in which utterances acquire wider social significance is through the *force* attaching to the content a speaker expresses. By 'force' we mean the kind of speech act the speaker is performing, which modulates how the meaning being expressed should be taken. For instance, an utterance of 'Please close the window' can be used to express different kinds of speech act in different contexts. In one context, it might constitute a polite request but in another (where the speaker occupies a higher social role or a position of power) it might constitute an order. Or again, 'I will give you £5' might simply be a description of my probable future behaviour, or it might constitute a promise, something I am committed (simply via the speech act of promising) to doing and which I can be held culpable for not doing.

When thinking about speech acts, and how force modulates what a speaker is taken to mean, it seems that there are two core lines for investigation: first, we need to know about the range of speech acts there are (including acts like stating, requesting, commanding, and promising). Second, we need to know what is required to successfully perform any given speech act, and what goes wrong when people fail to perform the speech act they want or intend to perform.

Both questions were explored at length by the Oxford philosopher J. L. Austin (and by others who pursued the kind of 'Ordinary Language Philosophy' he spearheaded). To answer the first question, Austin conducted a forensic examination of the way in which certain words get used in ordinary language and he employed this to generate a nuanced understanding of the range of different kinds of speech acts people perform.

Austin was also interested in the second question, of what is required to successfully perform a speech act and what goes wrong when we fail to perform the speech act we intend to. (This question has come to the fore recently, in contemporary debates about the use of language and the meanings that speakers are able to communicate in oppressive or unjust situations. For instance, as discussed in Chapter 2, philosophers like Jennifer Hornsby and Rae Langton have appealed to notions from Speech Act theory to explain the way in which women's voices may be silenced in certain contexts.) Austin argued that speech acts can go awry in two distinct ways, which he termed 'misfires' and 'abuses'. An example of a misfire occurs when I try to perform a given speech act which I lack the authority to perform. So, if an ordinary layperson announces to two people 'I now pronounce you man and wife' they will fail, thereby, to marry them, because they lack the authority required to perform the intended speech act (or, in Austin's terminology, the 'illocutionary act' of performing a marriage).

Sometimes, however, a speaker may be able to perform the speech act in question but do so in a way that is infelicitous (leading to what Austin says is 'an act professed but hollow'). If I say 'I promise I will give you £5' but in fact I have absolutely no intention of keeping this promise, one of the felicity conditions for promising is missing. This counts as an abuse of the speech act of promising.

In sum, whereas it seems quite plausible that occasion-specific speaker meaning can be analysed in terms of an individual's communicative intentions, it remains unclear whether the standing meanings of our words and sentences, and what we can use them to do, will be reducible to the psychological states of speakers or hearers.

Chapter 7
Meaning and use

Imagine the following encounter: you enter a café, smile broadly at the barista who is grinding coffee behind the counter, and say, 'Good morning.' What is the meaning of your utterance? Are you making a claim about the world, that is, that the morning is a good one? Do your words express a thought you have in mind, that is, that you hope the barista will have a good morning? Neither of these suggestions seems quite right. It seems far more plausible that you are simply performing an everyday greeting. But how do we fit greetings into a theory of meaning? And greetings are not the only example of speech that is difficult to analyse in terms of its relation to external objects or internal ideas. Consider, for example, 'please', 'thank you', 'sorry', and all sorts of other quite ordinary expressions. These examples, on top of the problems we encountered with referential and intentional theories of meaning in the preceding chapters, have led some thinkers to approach things from an entirely different angle.

In the last chapter, we began to distinguish between the kinds of meaning which are attributable to the intentions of individuals, speaking on particular occasions, and those which depend on the conventions adopted by larger social units (from groups of speakers to entire linguistic communities). This begins to suggest that meaning in language might emerge from what speakers are using their words for—that capturing meaning entails capturing use. Perhaps it is just misguided to look for a separate entity (like an object, idea, or communicative intention) that stands behind a word or a sentence and acts as its meaning. Some philosophers have proposed instead that all there is to meaning is how people use words and sentences, in the course of going about their daily business.

Meaning and functions

The slogan that 'meaning is use' is closely associated with the later thought of the philosopher Ludwig Wittgenstein (in a departure from his earlier work, which we encountered in Chapter 4). Wittgenstein compares words to tools:

> Think of the tools in a tool-box: there is a hammer, pliers, a saw, a screw-driver, a rule, a glue-pot, glue, nails and screws.—The functions of words are as diverse as the functions of these objects.

According to Wittgenstein, we shouldn't expect all of our words to map to meanings in a uniform way. Different words afford different sorts of possibilities, in the sense that we can use them to do different sorts of things. Just as there is nothing that unites the functions of hammers, saws, glue, etc., so there is nothing—no 'meaning-entity'—that unites the functions of names, colour terms, greetings, etc. Wittgenstein's suggestion is that, just as tools are made meaningful to us in virtue of their functions, so we can discover what words and sentences mean by looking at what they are used to do. Rather than trying to hook them directly onto things in the world or thoughts in people's heads, we should examine the roles they play in human activities. But this intriguing idea—that meaning in language consists in the uses we put it to—can still seem rather abstract and difficult to pin down.

One way to make the idea more concrete is to think about when (i.e. in which circumstances) people say the particular things they do. For example, most English speakers are inclined to say

'Good morning' when they believe that it is before 12 noon in their (or their interlocutor's) location and when they believe they are speaking to their interlocutor for the first time that day. We can think of these as conditions which license the utterance in its function as a greeting. By the same token, an utterance of 'Good morning' shapes how the linguistic interaction proceeds (with the audience typically responding in kind, or with another form of greeting).

Meaning in language, Wittgenstein held, can't be separated from the social activities we undertake using language, leading him to claim that 'speaking a language is part of an activity'. He noticed that our use of language in particular social contexts proceeds according to the rules or norms of the activity in which we are participating (be it building rapport with colleagues, teaching a class of students, or engaging in scientific debate, to name just a few possible examples). Thus, Wittgenstein spoke of the myriad 'language games' we play.

Individual language games might be thought of as social practices governed by norms and expectations, from which flow constraints on how words and sentences may be used (and, therefore, what may be meant by them). Thus, in our social practice of greeting, for example, 'Good morning' may be used until 12 noon (and 'Good afternoon' or 'Good evening' thereafter). At the most general level, whole languages like English, Portuguese, or Swahili might be thought of as complex language games, whose rules are deeply entangled with what Wittgenstein called the 'form of life' of their speakers (although exactly how we should understand this 'form of life' remains controversial).

Meaning and doing

So far, we have been focusing on which words and sentences people are, or should be, willing to use on particular occasions. But this is only part of the story, since language is also connected to all sorts of other (linguistic and non-linguistic) phenomena. Extending Wittgenstein's metaphor of the language game, the philosopher Wilfrid Sellars distinguished three kinds of 'moves' that speakers can make: language entry moves, language–language moves, and language exit moves.

Language entry moves are those which take us into language games. For instance, as infants acquire language, they become participants in a speech community and the language game of, say, English or Dutch. A more localized example would be starting to use the jargon of a particular discipline like quantum physics or literary studies, in order to engage in scholarly discussions in that area; or switching into the lexicon associated with a particular pursuit like rock-climbing or photography, when talking with other enthusiasts.

Language–language moves in turn allow us to make transitions of various kinds between sentences. For example, if the American President were to report, 'I have just returned from a very constructive visit to Beijing,' we would be licensed to assert things like 'The American President has been to China.' The idea here is very similar to the one we looked at in Chapter 5 under the heading of 'conceptual role semantics', except that here the focus is on entailment relations between sentences in language (rather than being couched directly at the level of thought). The view that word meanings depend on such relations is known as 'inferential role semantics'. The typical strategy is to start at the level of full sentences and then work out what individual words mean in terms of the relations between the different sentences in which the word appears. A somewhat similar approach, known as 'distributional semantics', has also proved extremely influential in the development of artificial language processing systems (such as ChatGPT and its very many predecessors). According to this approach, the meaning of an expression can be captured by analysing the statistical relations between it and all the other expressions of the language, for instance examining how often the word 'dog' is followed by 'barks' or 'bites' versus the words 'flies' or 'purrs'. (As noted in Chapter 1, this kind of approach was neatly summarized by J. R. Frith in 1957 with the aphorism, 'You shall know a word by the company it keeps.') Finally, language exit moves take us from within the language game to other kinds of non-linguistic activity that lie outside it. For instance, if you tell me, 'It has just started raining,' I might pick up my umbrella before leaving the house, or I might decide to catch the bus rather than walking to my destination. In this way, our participation in language games has real—and often very helpful—practical implications. Some forms of inferential (and conceptual) role semantics seek to accommodate these by conceiving of the functional role of a word or sentence very broadly, to include its non-linguistic causes and effects, alongside its linguistic ones. As we saw in Chapter 2, there can also be a darker side to this relationship between speech and the other kinds of action it engenders, for instance when we think about the use of propaganda or oppressive language and the unjust actions such language may engender.

Crucially, Wittgenstein thought that bits of language acquire meaning in virtue of how they are deployed in such games. He drew an analogy with the game of chess, comparing the pieces on a chess board with linguistic expressions or utterances. Simply being able to label (or refer to) the different pieces on a chess board (as bishops, pawns, rooks, and so on) does not help much if we actually want to play the game; instead, we need to know how those pieces can be used to further the objective of capturing the other player's king (while protecting one's own). For example, we need to know that bishops can only move diagonally. Wittgenstein suggests that, just as a bishop is defined by its moving diagonally in the game of chess, so the meanings of words and sentences are distilled from the ways in which we use them when engaged in one or other language game.

Arguably it is not just how people actually use language that matters—nor even how they *would* do so in this or that circumstance—but rather how they *should* use language. So, for example, if I happen to think that mornings go on until 3 p.m., I may well say 'Good morning' to you (and all sorts of related things) between the hours of 12 noon and 3 p.m. But that would seem to be a mistake on my part (and one which would likely be met with puzzlement, amusement, or correction on yours). This points to a feature of language (sometimes referred to as its 'normativity') whereby some uses count as correct while others are incorrect. Many philosophers who focus on the use of language (such as the American thinker Robert Brandom) want to capture linguistic normativity. So, they look beyond individuals' potentially idiosyncratic speech behaviours and focus on uses of language which are *appropriate*, or sanctioned by the wider linguistic community in some sense.

Meaning and rules

The idea we have arrived at, then, is that meaning in language depends on use, which in turn depends on the rules of the language game we are playing—rules which end up determining what we can mean. However, seeking to identify the meaning of a word with its rule of use raises some complex philosophical issues. To begin to see this, consider the following sequence of numbers:

2, 4, 6, 8, 10 ...

What comes next in the sequence? Intuitively, the next number will be 12 (according to the rule of adding 2 to the previous number at each step). But why couldn't the rule be, for example, *add 2 to the previous number until you reach double figures and then add 4* (so that the next number in the sequence should be 14); or, *add 2 to the previous number for four steps, then subtract 2 for two steps, and then repeat* (meaning we should write in 8 next in this list)?

Inspired by comments made by Wittgenstein, this puzzle was investigated in detail by the philosopher Saul Kripke (and is therefore sometimes attributed to 'Kripkenstein'). In general terms, the worry is that it is entirely indeterminate which rule is in force on any given occasion: since everything that has happened so far is consistent with infinitely many different rules, there is just no answer to the question of which rule is in force.

This worry arises with respect to meaning, in that all uses of a word or sentence so far seem consistent with infinitely many different rules determining how it should be used in the future. The problem is not just that we have no way to tell which rule is the right one but that there is simply no fact of the matter at all (because remember that all we are supposed to need on this account is facts about use; we are not supposed to 'look into the minds of speakers', as it were, and try to discern what rule they intended to follow). The best we can hope for is that, as language use unfolds, we can discard some possibilities. Even so, this still leaves indefinitely many others in play.

For instance, insofar as the sequence of numbers above continued with 12 we could reject a rule like *add 2 to the previous number until you reach double figures and then add 4*. But the following alternative rules would still be possible: *add 2 to the previous number until you reach treble figures and then add 4*; or, *add 2 to the previous number for five steps, then subtract 2 for two steps, and then repeat*. As for rule-governed sequences, so for meaning in language. After all, there is nothing to stop a phrase like 'Good morning' having the following rule of use: *use as a greeting before 12 noon until there have been three female presidents of the USA and then replace with 'Great morning'*. All we can do, then, is wait and see how words actually get used and how other members of the community react, that is, whether or not they accept these uses as permissible.

This idea that language gives us somewhat constrained but still very open-ended possibilities is inherent in Wittgenstein's

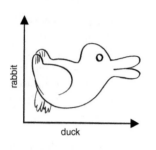
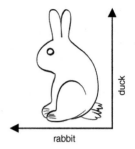

10. Wittgenstein's famous 'duck–rabbit' example.

portrayal of words as tools. While a hammer helps us to apply force to something, and pliers help us gain a tight grip, there are potentially infinitely many things we could use each tool to do. One day, for example, I could be hammering a nail into the wall in order to hang a picture; the next I could be banging on the walls in an attempt to alert my neighbour to the fact that I am trapped in the cellar, or I could be playing a makeshift drum in a local scrapheap band, or anything in between. Or again, the way that we interpret an image can change depending on what we think is relevant in it—Wittgenstein's famous example of the 'duck-rabbit' image being a case in point (see Figure 10). So, what is a tool really for? What does a word really mean?

Meaning and (in)stability

The sorts of indeterminacy worries introduced above have left some philosophers doubtful that the project of attributing standing meaning to linguistic expressions is actually viable at all. An example of a recent philosopher who takes this view is Charles Travis, who argues that it is only possible to talk about what a word or sentence meant on some particular occasion, once we have a rich appreciation of its role in an extended social interaction. Here is one of the examples Travis asks his readers to think about:

Pia's Japanese maple is full of russet leaves. Believing that green
is the colour of leaves, she paints them. Returning, she reports,
'That's better. The leaves are green now.' She speaks truth.
A botanist friend then phones, seeking green leaves for a study of
green-leaf chemistry. 'The leaves (on my tree) are green,' Pia says.
'You can have those.' But now Pia speaks falsehood.

What is meant by 'green' each time Pia utters it depends on
the purpose of the communicative exchange in which she is
participating: insofar as Pia is concerned with the tree *looking
green*, she may perfectly well describe the leaves as 'green' after
painting them. However, when it is the tree's natural properties
that are at issue, this suddenly seems inappropriate. What 'green'
means when someone utters it, then, seems to depend on what is at
stake in the conversation. Only when such facts are available,
Travis suggests, can the utterance be successfully interpreted.

Even once all the facts are in, Travis observes that individuals might
still disagree or be mistaken about the meaning of an uttered word
or sentence. In this scenario, Travis suggests that they would need
to turn to 'reasonable judges' to rule on the matter. It is not entirely
clear, though, who these judges should be. Travis suggests that, if
they are well-trained members of the linguistic community, ordinary
speakers can serve as reasonable judges, but it isn't at all obvious
that this would eliminate the possibility of error or disagreement.

In the example of Pia and the leaves, there does at least seem to be
something common to the uses of 'green', namely that the leaves
should be within a particular range on the colour spectrum, either
before or after painting (although we might still worry that there
will be some vagueness about exactly where to separate green from
other colours). But what if we were to come up with cases where
there is no common factor?

In Chapter 5 we briefly considered polysemous words like 'book',
which can be thought of as meaning either a physical object or its

content. Another example is 'window', which can be used to talk about an empty space (as in 'The window needs to be boarded up') or the glass that fills it (as in 'Can you clean the window so I can see out?'), or perhaps just the opening part (as in 'Sorry it's so hot in the glasshouse but the windows are tiny').

One worry when we think about polysemy is that there might be commonalities between multiple senses without all of them sharing a common core. For example, window-as-glass and window-as-opening-part might share the property of being solid, while 'window-as-empty-space' does not; yet 'window-as-empty-space' and 'window-as-opening-part' might share the property of enabling ventilation, while 'window-as-glass' does not (at least, not necessarily).

Wittgenstein seems to have had this kind of possibility in mind when he talked about 'family resemblances' between the different senses, or uses, of a word. We can imagine a family in which fraternal twins share their father's bushy eyebrows, while one shares the mother's blue eyes with a third sibling (who perhaps in turn shares her small stature with the other twin). Each sibling shares a feature with at least one of the others, even though no feature is common to all. Analogously, according to Wittgenstein, each use of a word may share a meaning property with at least one of the other uses, even though there is no meaning property that is common to all.

This shows just how radically the idea that meaning is use can upset our view of words and sentences as having broadly stable meanings. The view of language we end up with when we go down this route is one which sees the meanings of words as being extremely open-ended, dependent on all sorts of wider contextual factors, and interpretable only by suitably sensitive and sophisticated judges who are embedded in particular linguistic activities or language games. That leaves us with some problems. Currently, we have little idea of how to build rich contextual information into our models of meaning, so as to make sense of what a sophisticated judge—let alone a perfectly ordinary language-user—could be doing when producing and understanding speech. Yet previously we attributed the ability of humans to produce and understand all kinds of entirely novel sentences to the knowledge speakers have of a finite number of word meanings and some rules for putting together (or composing) those basic words into meaningful phrases and sentences. How can we account for this ability (which we labelled 'the productivity of language') now, if so little information is carried by language itself, and so much by the wider context? This is a question we will have to answer if we choose to pursue the idea that meaning is to be found in use.

Meaning and convention

We have seen how shining a light on language use can give greater prominence to the role of social norms and practices in shaping meaning. We already began to see this in the previous chapter, when we considered how speakers might make use of widespread assumptions about the nature of communication (e.g. that speakers can be expected to be truthful, informative, and relevant) to get information across (by way of 'implicatures') or to effect real changes in our social, legal, or moral relations (by undertaking different 'speech acts'). For example, when people say 'I do' in the context of wedding ceremonies, they only change their legal status because of society's conventions around getting married—and not (just) because they intend to do so. Without the utterance being embedded within these convention-based practices, it would end up meaning something different (if it meant anything at all).

Some philosophers believe that conventions are responsible for even larger swathes of the meanings we express through language. Recently, linguists and philosophers including Ernie Lepore, Matthew Stone, and Una Stojnic have argued that many apparently speaker-intended meanings are really driven by linguistic (or other) rules.

One example Lepore and Stone think about involves an utterance of 'Can you play Chopin's E minor prelude?' On the standard Gricean view we explored in the previous chapter, this is literally a question about whether the addressee is capable of playing that musical piece. However, assuming it is common knowledge between the interlocutors that the addressee *is* capable, and if the context is suitable (say, there is a piano nearby), the utterance is quite likely to be reinterpreted as an indirect request. In other words, it can be thought of as carrying an implicature with a content like 'Please play Chopin's E minor prelude'.

Lepore and Stone reject this analysis, arguing instead that 'Can you…' is a perfectly conventional way of making a request in English, such that the sentence 'Can you play Chopin's E minor prelude' is simply ambiguous between an enquiry about the addressee's capabilities and a request to play the piece. In a similar vein, they try to show that many meanings previously thought to be figured out 'on the fly' are actually baked into the language itself, or into the conventional ways in which we use it. If this were correct, speakers and hearers would be largely relieved of the need to reason about each other's communicative intentions and associated mental states. Instead, they could rely much more heavily on their knowledge of the conventions of language.

In some respects, this convention-focused view takes us back to a much older 'code model' of communication, associated with the linguists Ferdinand de Saussure and Roman Jakobson, which preceded modern investigations into the pragmatics of speech. In seeing facts about language use as integral to meaning, this view is also akin to the Wittgensteinian ideas we explored earlier in the chapter. However, in other ways the views are fundamentally at odds—whereas the Wittgensteinians open up issues of radical indeterminacy and instability, those who champion conventions seek to bring meaning back within the grasp of theorizing. A recurring concern with such approaches, though, is that they fail to capture the genuine flexibility language allows us. (Lepore and Stone attempt to reinstate this by complementing their appeal to conventions with an appeal to *human imagination*, to explain the more creative aspects of meaning and communication.)

What meaning is and where meaning comes from

We have looked at a range of different answers to the fundamental questions of what meaning is and where meaning comes from, exploring the idea that signs become meaningful through their connection with things in the world (Chapters 3 and 4), through their connection with thoughts and minds (Chapters 5 and 6), and through the way they are used (this chapter). Each of the approaches we encountered attempted to explain what it is for words or sentences (along with signs, symbols, and a range of other meaningful phenomena) to mean what they do. So, which is the most promising route to a robust and comprehensive theory of meaning? Like many of the thinkers we have discussed, you might find yourself strongly drawn towards one or other account—finding it intuitively appealing to think of meaning as emerging from the connection between a sign and an element of the world, or of thought, or of use. Yet, as we have seen, each approach comes with a variety of drawbacks (as well as attractions).

Alternatively, then, you might think there are ways to combine the best parts of multiple accounts. For example, referential theories seem to do a good job of explaining how sentences can be true or false, and why language works so well as a system for conveying information about the world, while intentional theories may help us much more when thinking about pragmatic meaning and the cut-and-thrust of communication. Or again, while the meanings of some expressions seem to be best explained by appeal to the speech acts we use them to perform, like greeting, apologizing, or making promises, others may have much closer connections to objects or ideas.

As we have seen here with respect to meaning in language, which source we focus on will have repercussions for how we think about questions of meaning. A focus on connections with the external world imports notions of truth and reference, suggesting an objective and shared perspective on meaning. This kind of perspective is likely to stress the role that rules play in generating claims of meaning, searching for the predictable, repeatable processes (either at the level of thought or language) which explain how we are able to grasp the meaning of novel signs, including new combinations of words. This external perspective is also likely to resist the idea that meaning can be relativized to individuals and to reject what is sometimes known as the 'post-truth' dialogue (where objective facts are held to be less important in shaping public understanding than feelings or personal responses) which follows from any such relativization.

On the other hand, focusing on the mental realm as grounding meaning suggests a more subjective approach. (Though, if we can make sense of the idea, defended by some philosophers, that concepts and thoughts are things which can be shared or common across multiple thinkers, it doesn't *demand* a subjective turn.) A more subjective approach to meaning might be thought to resonate with an influential strand in contemporary debate which emphasizes the importance of lived experience and personal response prior to settling questions of meaning. Such a perspective is also likely to stress the indirect content that our signs and symbols may carry, helping to make us more sensitive to the potentially oppressive and damaging ideas certain kinds of signs (or even entire language games) may carry with them.

Finally, an emphasis on role, purpose, or practice in fixing meaning chimes with the kind of debates we have explored in this chapter, where we ask about the practical repercussions of assigning this or that meaning to some sign, seeking a better understanding of the norms and conventions in play in our society. Perhaps a single one of the approaches we have looked at provides the unique right account of meaning in language, or perhaps some combination is needed, or maybe we should appeal to one or another dependent on context. The deep philosophical debates are likely to continue, because, as we have seen, the view of meaning we adopt *matters*.

References

Chapter 1: Meaning and language

We quote the opening lines of P. F. Strawson's lecture 'Meaning and Truth'. The full text is available in a collection of Strawson's work entitled *Logico-Linguistic Papers*, originally published in 1971 by Ashgate Publishing and reissued in 2004 by Routledge (see chapter 9).

We discuss 'the Chinese Room' thought experiment from John Searle's 1980 article 'Minds, Brains and Programs', appearing in Volume 3 of the journal, *Behavioral and Brain Sciences* (pp. 417–57).

Charles Sanders Peirce's quote on signs comes from Volume 2 of *The Collected Papers of Charles Sanders Peirce*, edited by Charles Hartshorne and Paul Weiss and published by Harvard University Press in 1932.

We discuss Hilary Putnam's thought experiment about Churchill and the ants, which is taken from Putnam's 1981 book *Reason, Truth and History*, published by Cambridge University Press (see chapter 1).

In our discussion of Large Language Models, we mention a paper by Emily M. Bender, Timnit Gebru, Angelina McMillan-Major, and Shmargaret Shmitchell, called 'On the Dangers of Stochastic Parrots: Can Language Models Be Too Big?' which appeared in the Proceedings of the 2021 ACM Conference on Fairness, Accountability, and Transparency.

John Rupert Frith's slogan for distributional semantics comes from his 1957 paper 'A Synopsis of Linguistic Theory, 1930–1955', which appeared in the journal *Studies in Linguistic Analysis*.

W. V. O. Quine talks about 'the myth of the museum' in his essay 'Ontological Relativity', which is collected in his 1969 book entitled *Ontological Relativity and Other Essays*, published by Columbia University Press.

Chapter 2: Meaning and practical problems

The case inspired by Jennifer Saul comes from her 2002 paper 'What is Said and Psychological Reality: Grice's Project and Relevance Theorists' Criticisms', appearing in Volume 25 of the journal *Linguistics and Philosophy* (pp. 361–4).

Lynne Tirrell's discussion of propaganda in the Rwandan genocide comes from her essay 'Genocidal Language Games', which appeared in a 2012 book entitled *Speech and Harm: Controversies Over Free Speech*, edited by Ishani Maitra and Mary Kate McGowan and published by Oxford University Press. More general discussion of 'toxic speech' can be found in Tirrell's 2017 article 'Toxic Speech: Toward an Epidemiology of Discursive Harm', published in Volume 45 of the journal *Philosophical Topics*.

The late Justice Antonin Scalia, who wrote the majority opinion verdict for the US Supreme Court's judgment in the landmark *District of Columbia v. Heller*, 554 U.S. 570 (2008) held that the Second Amendment to the US Constitution protects an individual's right to bear arms unconnected with service in a militia since the phrase 'to bear arms' did not refer to military contexts in the founding era. This claim is rejected by Dennis Baron in his 2018 paper 'Corpus Evidence Illuminates the Meaning of Bear Arms', published in *Hastings Constitutional Law Quarterly* 46, 509.

<https://heinonline.org/HOL/Page?handle=hein.journals/hascq46&div=20&g_sent=1&casa_token=dwFTDuK5SboAAAAA:RmWDEIDxwxHK_fHNcwqxZL6UOWghQ98CgTCDy53OKdBdPwJjZNM6vYvl_CbtZ5WC3_iThFjW&collection=journals>.

The quote by H. L. A. Hart comes from his 1958 article 'Positivism and the Separation of Law and Morals', appearing in Volume 71 of the journal *Harvard Law Review*.

Stephen Neale discusses the case of *Smith v. United States* (1993) in his 2007 article 'On location', in M. O'Rourke and C. Washington (eds), *Situating Semantics*. Cambridge, Mass.: MIT Press, pp. 251–393.

The first study of framing effects is reported by Amos Tversky and Daniel Kahneman in their 1981 paper 'The Framing of Decisions and the Psychology of Choice', appearing in Volume 211 of the journal *Science*.

Chapter 3: Meaning and objects

We cite John Stuart Mill's 1843 work *A System of Logic, Ratiocinative and Inductive*, Volume 1, Book II (entitled 'Of Names'), republished in 2012 by Cambridge University Press.

John Perry's example of the sugar trail in the supermarket comes from his 1979 article 'The Problem of the Essential Indexical', appearing in Volume 13 of the journal *Noûs* (pp. 3–21).

Saul Kripke's discussion of the name 'Aristotle' comes from his 1980 work *Naming and Necessity*, based on three lectures he delivered at Princeton in 1970 and published by Harvard University Press.

We discuss Gottlob Frege's example involving 'Hesperus' and 'Phosphorus', which comes from his 1892 German-language article 'Über Sinn und Bedeutung', appearing in Volume 100 of the journal *Zeitschrift für Philosophie und philosophische Kritik* (pp. 25–50). An English translation, entitled 'On Sense and Reference', is included in the book *Translations from the Philosophical Writings of Gottlob Frege*, edited by Peter Geach and Max Black, the 3rd edition of which was published by Blackwell in 1980.

Chapter 4: Meaning and truth

Ludwig Wittgenstein's *Tractatus Logico-Philosophicus* was first published in German in 1921. Notable English translations include that of C. K. Ogden (and F. P. Ramsey) in 1922, published by Routledge & Kegan Paul; and that of D. F. Pears and B. F. McGuinness in 1961, published by Humanities Press.

We cite Richard Montague's paper 'English as a Formal Language', which appeared in 1970 in a book entitled *Linguaggi nella societa e nella tecnica*, edited by Bruno Visentini (pp. 188–221). It was later reprinted in Montague's own book *Logic and Philosophy for Linguists*, published by De Gruyter Mouton in 1975.

Max Cresswell's 'Most Certain Principle' comes from his 1982 piece 'The Autonomy of Semantics', which appeared in the book *Processes, Beliefs, and Questions*, edited by Stanley Peters and Esa Saarinen and published by Reidel (pp. 69–86).

Hilary Putnam introduces his 'Twin Earth' thought experiment in a 1975 paper called 'The Meaning of Meaning', appearing in Volume 7 of the journal *Minnesota Studies in the Philosophy of Science* (pp. 131–93).

Chapter 5: Meaning and concepts

The quote from Jesse Lee Bennett is taken from his 1923 work *What Books Can Do for You: A Sketch Map of the Frontiers of Knowledge, with Lists of Selected Books*, published by George H. Doran company.

Steven Pinker's quote (attributed to Dan Dennett) appears in his 2008 book *The Stuff of Thought: Language as a Window into Human Nature*, published by Penguin.

We cite Lera Boroditsky's study of English and Mandarin speakers, from her 2001 article 'Does Language Shape Thought? Mandarin and English Speakers' Conceptions of Time', appearing in Volume 43 of the journal, *Cognitive Psychology* (pp. 1–22).

Chapter 6: Meaning and intentions

The implicatures we discuss are drawn from, or inspired by, H. P. Grice's paper on *Logic and Conversation*, collected in his 1989 work *Studies in the Way of Words*, published by Harvard University Press.

Examples of speech acts, misfires, and abuses are similarly drawn from, or inspired by, J. L. Austin's William James Lectures, delivered in 1955 and subsequently collected in *How To Do Things With Words*, the 2nd edition of which was edited by J. O. Urmson and Marina Sbisà, and published by Harvard University Press in 1975.

Chapter 7: Meaning and use

We quote Wittgenstein's comparison of words with tools, taken from Part I, Paragraph 11 of Ludwig Wittgenstein's *Philosophical Investigations*, translated by G. E. M. Anscombe and published for the first time by Macmillan in 1953 (with several other editions appearing later).

We quote a thought experiment from Charles Travis's 1997 essay on 'Pragmatics', which originally appeared in *A Companion to the Philosophy of Language*, edited by Bob Hale and Crispin Wright and published by Blackwell. The piece was subsequently included in Travis's 2008 collection *Occasion-Sensitivity: Selected Essays*, published by Oxford University Press.

Further reading

Good general introductions to many of the topics covered in this book include:

- Devitt, M. and Sterelny, K. 1987. *Language and Reality: An Introduction to the Philosophy of Language*, Blackwell.
- Hale, B. and Wright, C. (eds). 2017. *Blackwell Companion to the Philosophy of Language*, Blackwell Press.
- Lepore, E. and Sosa, D. (eds). 2019. *Oxford Studies in Philosophy of Language*, Oxford University Press, Volumes 1–3.
- Lepore, E. and Stojnić, U. (eds). Forthcoming. *The Oxford Handbook of Contemporary Philosophy of Language*, Oxford University Press.
- Lycan, W. 1999. *Philosophy of Language*, Routledge.

The Stanford Encyclopedia of Philosophy is an excellent online resource (<https://plato.stanford.edu/>). We highlight particularly relevant entries at the start of each chapter entry below.

Chapter 1: Meaning and language

Stanford Encyclopedia of Philosophy entries on: Word Meaning; the Turing Test; the Chinese Room Argument; Compositionality. See also Jaszczolt, K. M. 2023. *Semantics, Pragmatics, Philosophy: A Journey through Meaning*, Cambridge University Press; and Cappelen, H. and Dever, J. 2021. *Making AI Intelligible*, Oxford University Press.
More detailed and advanced coverage can be found in Jackendoff, R. 2002. *Foundations of Language: Brain, Meaning, Grammar,*

Evolution, Oxford University Press; Schlenker, P. 2022. *What it All Means: Semantics for (Almost) Everything*, MIT Press. Emma Borg explores the issues around artificial systems in her 'LLMs, Turing Tests and Chinese Rooms: The Prospects for Meaning in Large Language Models' in *Inquiry* 2024.

Chapter 2: Meaning and practical problems

Stanford Encyclopedia of Philosophy entries on: The Definition of Lying and Deception; Hate Speech; section 4.1 (Feminist Arguments against Pornography) in the entry on Pornography and Censorship; Legal Interpretation. See also Cappelen, H. and Dever, J. 2019. *Bad Language*, Oxford University Press.

More detailed and advanced coverage can be found in Anderson, L. and Lepore, E. (eds). Forthcoming. *The Oxford Handbook of Applied Philosophy of Language*, Oxford University Press; Fogal, D., Harris, D. W., and Moss, M. (eds). 2018. *New Work on Speech Acts*, Oxford University Press; Khoo, J. and Sterken, R. K. (eds). 2021. *The Routledge Handbook of Social and Political Philosophy of Language*, Routledge; Langton, R. 2009. *Sexual Solipsism: Philosophical Essays on Pornography and Objectification*, Oxford University Press; Maitra, I. and McGowan, M. K. (eds). 2012. *Speech and Harm: Controversies over Free Speech*, Oxford University Press; Saul, J. 2012. *Lying, Misleading, and What is Said: Exploration in Philosophy of Language and in Ethics*, Oxford University Press; and Stanley, J. 2015. *How Propaganda Works*, Princeton University Press.

Chapter 3: Meaning and objects

Stanford Encyclopedia of Philosophy entries on: Names; Reference; Gottlob Frege; Teleological Theories of Mental Content. See also Jorgensen, A. 2010. 'Scepticism about Meaning and Reference: Three Arguments by Quine, Putnam and Kripke', *Language and Linguistics Compass*, Volume 4, Issue 8, and Leahy, B. 2014. 'Teleosemantics: Intentionality, Productivity, and the Theory of Meaning', *Language and Linguistics Compass*, Volume 8, Issue 5.

Some important but more challenging primary texts include: Frege, G. 'On Sense and Reference' (extract in *Readings in Philosophy of Language*, ed. J. Hornsby and G. Longworth, Blackwell, 2006); Kripke, S. 1979. 'Speaker's Reference and Semantic Reference', in French, P. A., et al. (eds). *Contemporary Perspectives in the*

Philosophy of Language, University of Minnesota Press; Kripke, S. 1980. *Naming and Necessity*, Harvard University Press; Millikan, R. G. 2005. *Language: A Biological Model*, Clarendon Press.

Chapter 4: Meaning and truth

Stanford Encyclopedia of Philosophy entries on: Donald Davidson; Ludwig Wittgenstein; Externalism about the Mind.
More detailed and advanced coverage can be found in: Borg, E. 2004. *Minimal Semantics*, Oxford University Press; Davidson, D. 2001. *Inquiries into Truth and Interpretation*, Clarendon Press; Dummett, M. 1978. *Truth and Other Enigmas*, Harvard University Press; Montague, R. 1975. *Logic and Philosophy for Linguists*, De Gruyter Mouton; Partee, B. H. 2004. *Compositionality in Formal Semantics: Selected Papers*, Wiley-Blackwell; Wittgenstein, L. 1961. *Tractatus Logico-Philosophicus* (translated by D. F. Pears and B. F. McGuinness), Humanities Press.

Chapter 5: Meaning and concepts

Stanford Encyclopedia of Philosophy entries on: Concepts; Mental Representation; The Language of Thought Hypothesis. See also Borg, E. Forthcoming. 'The Problems of Polysemy', in Lepore, E. and Stojnić, U. (eds) *The Oxford Handbook of Contemporary Philosophy of Language*, Oxford University Press.
More detailed and advanced coverage can be found in: Fodor, J. 1975. *The Language of Thought*, Thomas Y. Crowell; Fodor, J. 1998. *Concepts: Where Cognitive Science Went Wrong*, Oxford University Press; Pustejovsky, J. and Boguraev, B. 1997. *Lexical Semantics: The Problem of Polysemy*, Oxford University Press.

Chapter 6: Meaning and intentions

Stanford Encyclopedia of Philosophy entries on: Paul Grice; Implicature; Pragmatics.
Some important primary texts include: Grice, H. P. 1991. *Studies in the Way of Words*, Harvard University Press; Sperber, D. and Wilson, D. 1995. *Relevance: Communication and Cognition* (2nd edn), Blackwell; Carston, R. 2002. *Thoughts and Utterances: The Pragmatics of Explicit Communication*, Wiley.

Chapter 7: Meaning and use

Stanford Encyclopedia of Philosophy entries on: John Langshaw
Austin (section 2 on 'Language and Truth'); Speech Acts; Meaning
Holism. See also Kissine, M. 2008. 'Locutionary, Illocutionary,
Perlocutionary', *Language and Linguistics Compass*, Volume 2,
Issue 6.

Some important primary texts include: Austin, J. L. 1975. *How to Do
Things with Words* (2nd edn), Harvard University Press; Lepore, E.
and Stone, M. 2014. *Imagination and Convention: Distinguishing
Grammar and Inference in Language*, Oxford University Press;
Searle, J. 1969. *Speech Acts: An Essay in the Philosophy of Language*,
Cambridge University Press; Travis, C. 2008. *Occasion-Sensitivity:
Selected Essays*, Oxford University Press; Wittgenstein, L. 1976.
Philosophical Investigations (3rd edn, translated by
G. E. M. Anscombe), Basil Blackwell.

Index

For the benefit of digital users, indexed terms that span two pages (e.g., 52–53) may, on occasion, appear on only one of those pages.

Meaning